Mr. Lock the Hatter
Went to Sea
The Battle of Trafalgar

BY

Dr K S Cliff

published by Dr K S Cliff, Kestrels, Drove Lane,
ALRESFORD SO24 9EX
email: lockledger@btopenworld.com

Author: Dr K S Cliff, 2005 ©

No part of this publication may be reproduced in any form,
including electronic formats and transmission,
without written permission from the publisher.
All rights reserved.

ISBN 0-9550388-0-4

printed by Gwasg Helygain Ltd
68-70 Kinmel Street, Rhyl LL18 1AW
01745 331411

INDEX

	Page
Foreword	3
A Brief History of Lock & Co Ltd: Hatters	4
Lord Nelson's Hats	7
Captain Hon Henry Blackwood	14
Captain Hon Thomas Bladen Capel	22
Captain Henry Digby	28
Captain Richard King	34
Captain Thomas Masterman Hardy	40
Capt Thomas Francis Fremantle	52
Captain James Nicoll Morris	58
Captain William Hargood	63
Naval Hats 1800-05	72

FOREWORD

At the Battle of Trafalgar (Trafalgar) on the 21st October 1805, Vice Admiral Lord Nelson's Fleet (Nelson) of thirty-three ships defeated a Franco-Spanish Fleet totalling forty ships. The facts about Trafalgar, Nelson's life and death are well documented. There would therefore seem to be little to add to the current lists of books about these events. However, there are still some small but significant pieces of information to be found, not least in some of the surviving legders of James Lock & Co Ltd, Hatters, of 6 St James's St, London (Locks).

This booklet brings together a brief outline of the lives of eight Captains who served with Nelson at Trafalgar. They all shared something else in common and with Nelson, namely, they were all at sometime customers of Locks. At Trafalgar Nelson and four of his captains were already customers. Nelson wore one of two hats with eyeshades that he had bought in August/September 1805 just prior to his hurried departure for the Mediterranean and Trafalgar. After Trafalgar four other Captains were to purchase their hats from Locks. Thus out of the 33 ships in Nelson's Fleet eight of his Captains were customers of Locks. These findings are a unique piece of social naval history and are recorded here to add that snippet of history that helps towards the completeness of the Nelson Era information.

I wish to acknowledge the kind help and encouragement of all my colleagues and associates at Locks and in particular Janet Taylor. I wish to express my thanks also to the staff of the Metropolitan Archives in London; to Ken Hutchinson for his superb drawings; to Dr Colin White for his help and advice; to my family for their encouragement; and to Guto Lloyd-Davies for his help and patience in publishing the booklet.

Dr K S Cliff,
Kestrels, Drove Lane, ALRESFORD SO24 9EX
2005

A BRIEF HISTORY OF LOCK & CO Ltd: HATTERS

My great-great-grandfather James Benning (Benning) was a London' hatter under the name of Lock & Co (Locks). He was born in 1819 and died in 1899. He inherited the business as an equal partner with Mr CR Whitbourn (Whitbourn) on the 1st of January 1872. Whitbourn was the nephew of Mr James Lock 111, the last of three generations of Mr Lock to own the business. The name, Lock & Co, remained on the fascia of his shop, as it does today.

Figure 1: James Benning Circa 1882.

The business was established in 1676 by Robert Davis (Davis) in rented premises on the west side of St James's Street. Davis was a Hatter and Hosier and built up a very successful business through the sale of "quality hats" to members of the Nobility, Naval and Military Officers. These, and other customers, many of whom had their

London' residences in the adjoining neighbourhood, formed the majority of his customers. Davis took his son Charles into the business, who, on the death of his father in 1696, succeeded to the business.

Charles Davis had no surviving sons, only a daughter Mary. He wished his business to continue after his death, so he sought a husband for Mary. In 1747 he apprenticed James Lock the son of a neighbour. James Lock served his apprenticeship, learned the mysteries of the Hatter's trade, then courted and married Mary Davis in 1757. Charles Davis now had an heir.

In 1759 Charles Davis died and James Lock inherited his father in law's business. He continued at the same premises until 24 June 1765 when he took a lease on No 6 St James's Street. The sign over the shop read: "James Lock" (James 1). His wife died early in their marriage and only a daughter, Mary, survived. However in 1773 a "natural son" James II was born. His father (James 1) took him into partnership as his rightful son in 1794 and James 11 took over the business in 1799 when his father retired. He was to meet and serve Lord Nelson.

James Lock 11 was not a 'natural businessman' and in 1809 he invited Robert Lincoln to join the business as a partner. He hoped that this gentleman would help restore the fortunes of the business. This was not to be and it was the efforts of James Lock 11's son James Lock 111 who managed to save the business. The Lock-Lincoln partnership was dissolved, James Lock 11 was 'pensioned off' and James Lock 111 and his younger brother George took over the business. George served an apprenticeship under James 111 and became the professional Hatter. James 111 was the accountant and businessman. The business flourished and in 1835 Benning joined the business. He was the youngest son of Mr William Benning a Shoe and Leather Merchant who had supplied goods to Locks for many years.

Benning proved to be a very able young man, quick to learn and very good with customers. By his own merits he rose through the shop' hierarchy to become foreman. George and James Lock thought very highly of him. George Lock died suddenly leaving no heirs, and in his Will he left a legacy to Benning "in appreciation of his loyalty". James Lock 111 was unmarried and was faced with the decision as to what to do with the business. He invited his nephew, Charles Richard Whitbourn (Whitbourn), to join him as a partner; and then invited Benning to join them to form a triumvirate.

Whilst Whitbourn was taught the financial and administrative aspects of the business, Benning took George Lock's role as the Hatter. On the 31 December 1871 James Lock 111 retired and an era of a Mr Lock owning the business ceased after 112 years. However, this was not the end of the persona of the Mr Locks, for Benning took on that role. Whitbourn retired behind his office door and ran the financial side of the business to Benning's complete satisfaction. The name on the fascia over the front of the shop remained "Lock & Co". In 1913, No 6 St James's Street, which had been rented since 1765, was bought for £10,000. The property extended from St James's Street through to Crown Passage, and now included the cottage where the former owners had lived. This provided additional accommodation for the business, though there had always been a right of access from the shop to Crown Passage. In 1928 the business became a private limited company, James Lock & Co Ltd. Today the descendants of Benning and Whitbourn continue to own and run the business. (1)

REFERENCES

(1) Whitbourn, F. MR LOCK OF ST JAMES'S STREET. His Continuing Life and Changing Times. London: Heinemann, 1971. pp2-3
I wish to acknowledge the generosity of my dear friend Frank Whitbourn for allowing me to use sections from his book in this chapter.

LORD NELSON'S HATS

Nelson's first visit to Locks was on Tuesday 11th November 1800. After meeting James Lock 11 (Mr Lock) he discussed the type of hat he wanted. Mr Lock then measured round Nelson's head to ascertain his hat size. This was noted in the ledger as $7^{1}/_{8}$ Full. The term "full" indicated that he could take a generous sized $7^{1}/_{8}$ hat and possibly a "small $7^{1}/_{4}$". He placed an order for a Cocked Hat with Cockade. The hat was to be cocked "athwart", that was across the head rather than front to back. The hat was to be made of the finest Beaver Fur and the cockade and loop from navy-blue silk. Mr Lock would have asked if he wished to have any other embellishments, such as gold banding, gold lacing, or gold loop to hold the cockade. Nelson declined.

The cockade, with the loop placed over it, was attached to the hat by a button. This had a small threaded screw and nut incorporated on its underside. The button was inserted through the loop and cockade and then through the hat. Internally the screw and nut were covered with felt after tightening the nut to hold the cockade and loop firmly to the hat. Mr Lock would have provided the appropriate "anchor button" as required by the Admiralty' Dress Code. An account was arranged for Nelson coded as G or 9.563 according to the type of ledger. For example the Account' Ledger, recording all Nelson's entries, used the prefix G. Before the order was dispatched Mr Lock placed a patch on the inner lining of the hat to show that the "hat duty" had been paid. (William Pitt introduced this tax in 1783). Finally this order was sent to Nerot's Hotel.

On Tuesday 6th January 1801, Nelson visited Locks accompanied by his father the Rev Nelson. His father had retired from his "living" at Burnham Thorpe and, with Lady Nelson, had come to London to meet Nelson after his absence of nearly three years service with the Mediterranean Fleet. The Rev Nelson bought a Flapt Hat. This was a very popular style of round hat worn by the clergy. Basically this was a round Beaver Fur Hat with part of the sides turned up to form a small flap. Each flap was stiffened to stand up and curl slightly inwards. He paid 1/15/6 cash for the hat and took it with him.

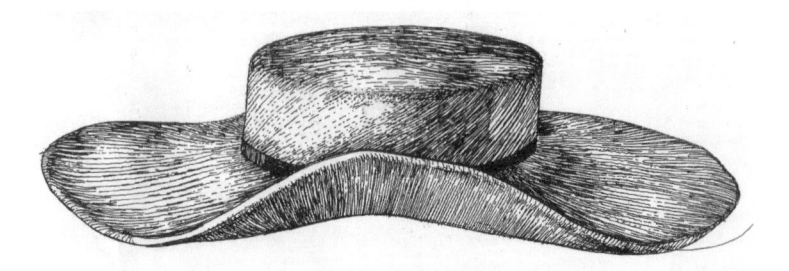

Figure 2. Flapt Clerical Hat.

Nelson placed a further order for a Cocked Hat and Cockade with a wooden box. Next day, 7th January 1801, Nelson collected the new hat and settled his account. He subsequently sailed to the Baltic with Admiral Sir Hyde Parker's Fleet and very possibly wore one or both hats during this period. Nelson returned to Locks on the 27th October 1801 and caused some surprise by announcing himself as the Duke of Bronte. After the Battle of the Nile on 2nd August 1798 Nelson spent some time at Naples protecting King Ferdinand of the Two Scillies and his family. For this and other services the King presented Nelson with an estate on the Island of Sicily close to Mount Etna. The estate was reputed to have an income of 3,000 pounds per year. With the estate came the title of 'Duke of Bronte'. This title was bestowed on Nelson with the lands on 13th August 1799. (1)

Nelson had to apply to His Majesty King George 111 for a licence to use this foreign title. This was granted on the 9 January 1801. (2) Nelson had been using the title in combination with his usual signature 'Nelson' before the latter date. He had tried Bronte & Nelson and other combinations, but decided on Nelson & Bronte" from about 5th February 1801 (3) Nelson ordered a new Cocked Hat with Cockade and Mr Lock entered the order in the Day Ledger as

"Duke of Bronti. The title was incorrectly spelt using an "i" instead of an "e".

During 1802 Nelson was to send for orders or visit my shop on a number of occasions. He was now based on a "Home Station". On the 19 January 1802 there was an order for two hats: "A Cocked Hat & Cockade" at 1/11/6; and a "Glazed Hat, with 1½ in Gold Band" at 1/7/-. This latter was for one of his household staff. The order was sent to No 23 Piccadilly, the London residence of Sir William and Lady Hamiliton. (4) He settled this account in the sum of 2/18/6 on the 7th July 1802. Following his summer tour of parts of England and Wales with Sir William and Lady Hamilton, Nelson visited Locks on the 6th and 8th September 1802. On the 6 September 1802 he ordered a new "Cocked Hat and Cockade" now priced at 1/14/- due to the rise in the price of Beaver Fur. He came to the shop on the 8 September 1802 to collect this hat and to order a Lady's Hat, probably for Lady Hamilton. He paid for both of these hats on the 9 September 1802.

On the 11 February 1803 Nelson's ordered the first, of what were to become his unique and distinguishing hats with green eyeshades. Nelson had had for some time problems with his eyes. He had lost the sight in his right eye at the siege of Bastia on the 12th July 1794. He had had and continued to suffer from bouts of inflammation in both eyes and from time to time his left eye (good eye) became covered with a thin inflammatory membrane. He had been advised to treat this by bathing his eyes with pure spring water and to wear an eyeshade. Nelson asked Mr Lock if he could make him a "Cocked Hat with a Green Shade attached". (5)

A sketch was made of the proposed hat, which Nelson accepted. The price for the hat was 2/2/-. This included: a stiffened shade covered with green silk, that shaded both eyes; and sewing the shade into the front of the hat. When not in use the shade could be turned up into the hat. Nelson returned the next day, 13th February 1803 and brought with him one of his previous hats that was to be re-cocked. He inspected the new hat and shade and ordered a spare shade. This was arranged at a price of 5/-. (From the existing ledgers at Locks it is not possible to ascertain whether this additional shade was taken as a spare, or attached to the re-cocked hat, probably the latter). Unusually Nelson did not settle his account.

Figure 3: Nelson's Cocked Hat and Eyeshade.

Nelson was then stationed in the Mediterranean for nearly two years, but before he left he made arrangements for certain named members of his household to use his account in his absence. This was quite usual if the lady of the house did not have a separate account. This authority was used to purchase a hat on the 3rd February 1805, when Lady Hamilton came into the shop to order a Midshipman's hat for Mr Charles Connor a relative of Lady Hamilton's. Nelson returned to England in August 1805 and visited Locks on the 20th Aug 1805. He ordered a new hat with eyeshade to be delivered to 11 Clarges Street.

He returned on the 24th August 1805 and ordered a spare green eyeshade and cockade.

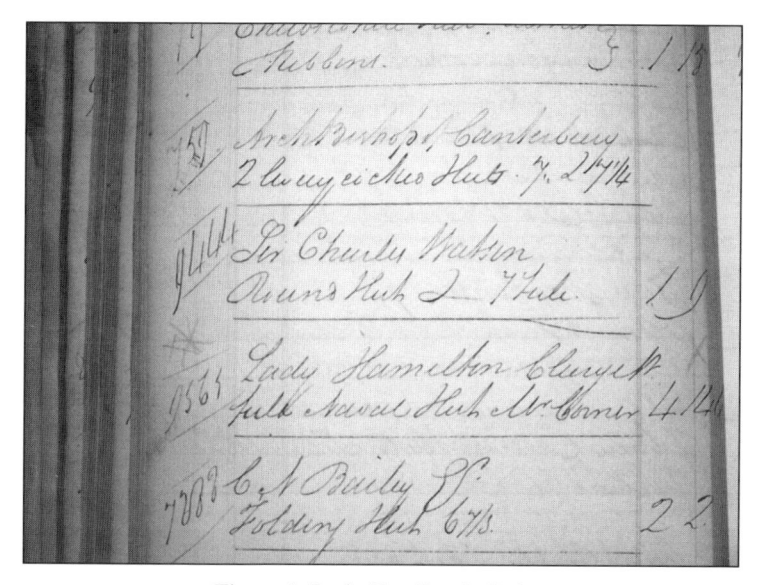

Figure 4: Lady Hamilton's Order.

On the 9th September 1805 he ordered another Cocked Hat and Cockade with Green Eyeshade to be delivered next day, again to 11 Clarges Street. On the morning of Friday 13 September 1805, Nelson came to Locks to pay his outstanding bill for Eleven pounds, nineteen shillings and sixpence. (That sum included the outstanding account from 1803). He then travelled to his country house at Merton in Surrey, and thence to Portsmouth. He sailed in his 100 Gun Flagship HMS Victory to the Mediterranean and his death at the Battle of Trafalgar on 21 October 1805.

Nelson wore one of the hats made by Locks before and during the Battle of Trafalgar. His dress on the Victory was recorded by one of his Lieutenants as: "…a plain cocked hat with a green eyeshade fixed to it over his right eye but worn nearly square". Not quite the correct description! (6) Further evidence that Nelson wore a Lock' hat at Trafalgar comes in the form of a sketch by Mr Arthur Devis. He was present when Dr Beatty, Victory's surgeon, performed the autopsy on Nelson's body after its return to England. Dr Beatty's account of Lord Nelson's death was published in 1806. This included a sketch by Mr Devis of his cocked hat with green eyeshade.

LORD NELSON'S ORDERS

1800
11th November 1800: Cocked Hat & Cockade 7^1/$_8$th Full 1/11/6. (Sent to "Nerots Hotel", King Street, St James's.)

1801
6th January 1801: Cocked Hat & Cockade; Wood Box 4/-. 1/15/6. (Address not recorded. Known to be 17 Dover Street from his father's entry January 8 1801.)
7th January 1801: Paid his account in sum of: 3/7/- for 1800-01.
27th October 1801: Cocked Hat & Cockade. 1/11/6. Entry reads: "Duke of Bronti". G563

1802
19th January 1802: Cocked Hat & Cockade. 1/11/6: Glazed Hat, gold band 1½ in. 1/7/-. To 23 Piccadilly.
7th July 1802: Paid Account in sum of: 2/18/6 for orders of 19th January 1802
6th September 1802: Cocked Hat & Cockade. 1/14/- No address given.
8th September 1802: Lady's Black Hat, Rich Ostrich feather & elastic band. 2/12/6
This entry can only be found in the Account's Ledger under G563.
9th October 1802: Paid Account in sum of: 4/6/6 for September 1802's orders.

1803

11th February 1803: Cocked Hat, Cockade & Green Eyeshade. 2/2/-. First order for this type of hat.

12th February 1803: Cocked Hat put in shape: Green Shade 5/-. (The Account came to 2/7/-: Nelson paid in 1805.)

1805

3rd February 1805: Full Dress Midshipman's Hat for Mr Connor. 4/14/6. (Relative of Lady Hamilton. See Figure 4).
20th August 1805: Cocked Hat, Cockade & Green Eyeshade. 2/6/0.
24th August 1805: Green Shade & Cockade. 6/-.
9th September 1805: Cocked Hat & Green Eyeshade. Size 7 Full. 2/6/-
13th September 1805: Paid Account in sum of: 11/19/6. This included the Account for 2/7/- from 1803.

One of the hats with the eyeshade made by Locks still exists and can be seen on the effigy of Nelson in Westminster Abbey Museum.

REFERENCES

1) Nicolas, Sir N. THE DISPATCHES AND LETTERS OF LORD NELSON, The Nicholas Edition. London: Chatham Publishing, 1997. Vol 111. p439 (Nicolas).

2) Nicolas, Vol 111. p440

3) Pryor, F. in White C.D. (Ed) THE NELSON COMPANION. Stroud: Royal Naval Museum Publications & Sutton Publishing Ltd. 1997. pp162-4

4) Oman, C. NELSON. London: Reprint Society, Hodder & Stoughton Ltd, 1950. p363

5) Cliff, K.S. MR LOCK: HATTER TO LORD NELSON AND HIS NORFOLK NEIGHBOURS. Norwich: Wendy Webb Publishing, 2000. pp23-35

6) Fabb, J & Cassin-Scott, J. UNIFORMS OF TRAFALGAR. London: Batsford Ltd, 1977. p21

CAPTAIN HON HENRY BLACKWOOD

Captain Hon Henry Blackwood (Blackwood) was born on the 27th December 1770. He was the 5th son of Sir John Blackwood Bt of Ballyleidy, County Down. In April 1781, aged 11 years Blackwood was placed in the 40 Gun Frigate HMS Artois as a Volunteer under Capt Macbride. The Artois was a newly built Frigate captured from the French Navy. In August 1781 Blackwood saw action at the Battle of Doggerbank.

He served under several captains between 1781 and 1790. His main teacher was Commodore Phillips Cosby on the 50 Gun Ship HMS Trinity part of the Mediterranean Fleet. In 1790 Blackwood was transferred to the 100 Gun Ship HMS Queen Charlotte as a Signalman Midshipman under Admiral Earl Howe. He began to specialise in signalling and on the 3rd November 1790 Howe promoted him Lieutenant and in 1791 he transferred to the 32 Gun Frigate HMS Prosperine as the Signal Lieutenant. At the end of 1791 he obtained leave to go to France. He returned at the end of 1792 to England and was appointed to the 38 Gun Frigate HMS Active. He then transferred as 1st Lieutenant to the 74 Gun Ship HMS Invincible by special request of the Captain, The Hon Thomas Pakenham. (1)

He was present on the HMS Invincible, during the chase of a French Fleet between the 18th May and 1st June 1794. The final action on the 1st June 1794 became known as the Battle of the Glorious 1st of June. Seven French ships were captured, though one later sank. Invincible was closely engaged and her crew suffered 14 killed and 31 wounded. (2) Blackwood was next appointed to the 12 Gun Fire-ship HMS Megaera first with Howe's and then Admiral Lord Bridport's Fleet. On the 2nd June 1795 Blackwood was promoted to Captain. He stayed with Bridport's Fleet and was present at the action off Groix on 23 June 1795.

Blackwood saw little further action. He commanded a Guard-Ship at Hull until his appointment to the 28 Gun Frigate HMS Brilliant. He served in her first as part of Admiral Duncan's North Sea Fleet, then on the Newfoundland Station as part of Admiral Waldegrave's Fleet and finally to the Mediterranean Fleet. On the 26th July 1798 Blackwood sighted two 36 Gun French Frigates the Regeneree and Vertu at anchor in Tenerife. They too sighted Blackwood and the French ships gave chase. The Regeneree brought the Brilliant to action but was considerably damaged in the engagement. The Vertu then sought action but in the ensuing darkness Blackwood was able to escape. He returned to England in the spring of 1799 and transferred to the 36 Gun Frigate HMS Penelope. He first joined the Channel Fleet and then the Mediterranean Fleet.

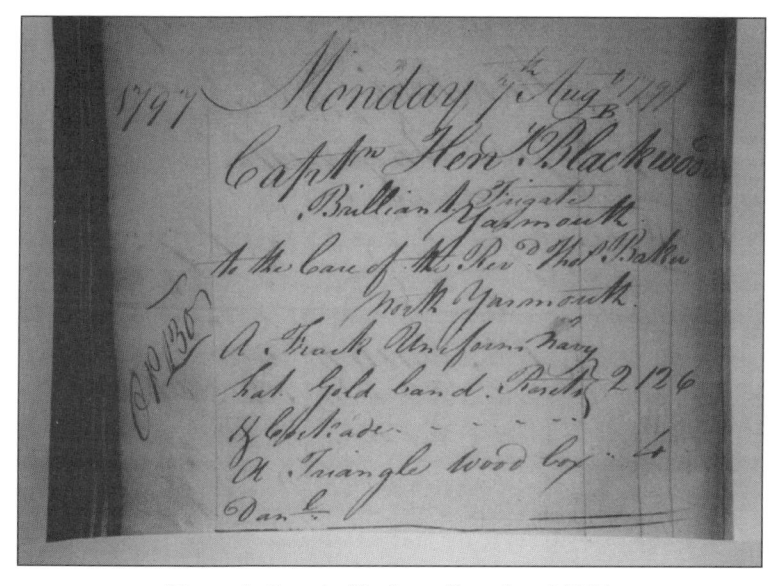

Figure 5: Captain Blackwood's order of 1797.

He took part in the blockade of Malta during the winter of 1799 and spring of 1800 as part of Captain Manely Dixon's Squadron. On the night of the 30th March 1800 the 80 Gun French Ship Guillaume Tell attempted to run the blockade in rough weather. She made sail and got outside the harbour but was seen by the watchful Blackwood and his crew. Blackwood sent the 16 Gun Sloop HMS Minorca to alert Capt Manely Dixon in the 60 Gun Ship HMS Lion. Blackwood in the Penelope followed the Guillaume Tell and attacked her repeatedly, badly damaging her. This allowed time for the Lion and the 80 Gun Ship HMS Foudroyant to engage her. The French vessel, after a long action, eventually struck her flag. However, the superb seamanship of Blackwood and the gunnery of the crew of the Penelope was a major factor in the capture of the Guillaume Tell. The Penelope suffered one crew' member killed and 3 wounded. The French ship was taken into Syracuse by Blackwood, and eventually into the British Navy as HMS Malta. (3)

Blackwood continued in the Mediterranean as part of Nelson's Squadron. Nelson gave him considerable discretion within his orders. He was sent by Nelson to watch for the enemy fleet between Capes' Spartel and St Vincent. (4) Blackwood remained in the Mediterranean until the declaration of the "Peace of Amiens" on 12th October 1801. The actual treaty was not signed until the 27 March 1802.

HMS Penelope was "paid off" and Blackwood was on shore until war broke out again in April 1803. This time was one of sadness for Blackwood. He and his second wife Elizabeth had taken a house at Catisfield near Fareham in Hampshire. On the 30th October 1802 Elizabeth died and was buried at St Peter's Church Titchfield on the 2nd November 1802.

With the resumption of war, Blackwood commissioned the new 36 Gun Frigate HMS Euryalus and served with the Channel Fleet. In July 1805 he was posted to the Mediterranean as part of Nelson's Fleet watching for the Franco-Spanish Fleet. In August 1805 Nelson returned to England and left Vice-Admiral Collingwood in command. He had a small squadron of ships watching Cadiz but in late August a superior force of the French and Spanish navies forced him away and entered into Cadiz. Collingwood ordered Blackwood to sail immediately for England with dispatches and the news of the enemies' fleet to the Admiralty in London.

Blackwood landed in England on the 2nd September 1805 but before going to the Admiralty he went directly to Merton House the home of Nelson. He arrived about 05-00 in the morning, gave the news to Nelson and then went on to London. Nelson followed shortly after. At the Admiralty Nelson was given his orders to sail immediately. Blackwood stayed in England until Nelson was ready to sail. They departed on 15th September 1805 from Portsmouth, Nelson in his Flagship the 100 Gun Ship HMS Victory and Blackwood in Euryalus. (5)

Nelson appointed Blackwood to the command of an Inshore Squadron to be the "eyes and ears" of the fleet. Blackwood was offered the appointment as Captain of a Ship of the Line but refused. He organised his small but fast fleet so that as far as possible they were in signal range of one with another at all times. He was able to report the daily activity of the combined enemy fleet to Nelson. This fleet eventually sailed from Cadiz on the 20th October 1805. Blackwood had relayed the news to Nelson and on the morning of the 21st October 1805 was aboard the Victory when Nelson gave the order to engage the enemy. He was still on board when the opening shots were fired against the Victory. With Captain Hardy he witnessed Nelson's signature on a Codicil to his Will. As he left the Victory to return to Euryalus Nelson shook him by the hand and said: "God bless you, Blackwood, I shall never speak to you again".

Blackwood was of the opinion that Nelson had given him command of: All the Frigates at Trafalgar to assist disabled ships; and to use Nelson's name to do "what struck him best" in the use of the rearmost

Ships of the Line". Whether this was correct was never tested during the Battle but his thoughts were set out in a letter to his wife immediately after the battle. (6) After the battle Collingwood transferred his flag to the Euryalus for about 10days and then to HMS Queen. He then sent Blackwood to England with dispatches and the captured French Admiral, Vice-Admiral Villeneuve. On his return to England he reported to the Admiralty; and then attended Nelson's Funeral on the 9th January 1806 as "Train Bearer" to Admiral of the Fleet Sir Peter Parker the Chief Mourner.

Post Trafalgar

After Nelson's Funeral Blackwood returned to the Mediterranean in the 74 Gun HMS Ajax and rejoined Collingwood's Fleet on the 21st October 1806. He was subsequently seconded to join Vice-Admiral Sir John Duckworth's Squadron, ordered to sail for the Dardanelles. On the night of the 14 February 1807 the Ajax caught fire and eventually blew up. Blackwood survived but many of his crew were lost. He joined Duckworth's 100 Gun Flag Ship HMS Royal George and returned to England. In May 1807 he took command of the 74 Gun Ship HMS Warspite and served with the North Sea Fleet.

He returned to the Mediterranean and in 1810 was appointed to the command of an Inshore Squadron off Toulon. On the 20th July 1810 Blackwood's Squadron was in a successful action against the French Fleet when it attempted to leave Toulon, and drove them back into port. In 1812 he retuned to England and remained in charge of the Warspite until 1813. In 1814 he was given a special appointment as Captain of the Fleet under the Duke of Clarence (William 1V) on the visit of some of the Crowned Heads of Europe allied to Britain. For this service he was awarded a Baronetcy. On the 4th June 1814 he was appointed Rear-Admiral. In 1819 he was nominated KCB and also C in C East Indies serving until December 1822. He was appointed Vice-Admiral on 27th May 1825 and C in C Nore from 1827 to 1830.

He died on the 17th December 1832 at Ballyleidy in Ireland near where he was born.

Nelson Correspondence

Investigations of the naval literature revealed little personal correspondence between Nelson and Blackwood, other than on Naval Matters. This is evident in the letters sent especially during October 1805. At that time Blackwood, with his inshore squadron, watched the Franco-Spanish Fleet in Cadiz. In a letter of the 9th October 1805 Nelson asked Blackwood to remember him: "..to all the Captains of Blackwood's Inshore Squadron". (7)

One personal letter to Blackwood is of considerable interest. When Nelson wrote it he had not yet met Blackwood but only heard of his exploit in bringing the French Ship Guillaume Tell to be captured. The capture and subsequent transfer to the Royal Navy as HMS Malta was of great satisfaction to Nelson as now the entire French Nile Fleet had been destroyed or captured.

In the letter dated 5 April 1800 sent to Blackwood from Palermo, Nelson speaks of his belief of a sympathy that can bind people together in the bonds of friendship without having a personal knowledge of each other. He expresses his belief that there was such a bond between himself and Blackwood. He wrote: "I was your friend and acquaintance before I saw you". (8) Blackwood's standing in the Royal Navy was further enhanced in correspondence from Commissioner Isaac Coffin to Nelson dated 24 Aug 1799. Coffin was an old friend of Nelson's and wrote to say that if he recommended a friend to him (Nelson) he could be sure he (Coffin) had a high opinion of that friend. Blackwood was such a friend. (9)

Later events showed the trust that Nelson put in Blackwood to carry out his orders and understand his strategy was not displaced.

Blackwood was to reciprocate their close Friendship on 2nd September1805. Collingwood had sent him to the Admiralty in London with dispatches and the news that the Franco-Spanish Fleet was in Cadiz. However, on arrival in England, he went first to Nelson at his home at Merton with the news, then to the Admiralty. He was one of the last Captains to leave the Victory as the Battle of Trafalgar started, having been a co-witness with Captain Hardy to Nelson's Codicil to his Will. Later he and Hardy were closely involved at Nelson's funeral. (10)

Hats from Lock & Co

BLACKWOOD Capt: Navy. 14 Mar/15 June 1795: Round Hat, 1/3/0; Cockt Hat Cockade: Wood box, 1/9/6.// Prince of Wales Coffee House. Cockt Hat: Cockade, 1/7/6.

BLACKWOOD Capt Hy: Navy: 10 July/ 7 Aug 1797. Queen Anne St Westminster. Bedford Hat.// Full Uniform Hat, Gold Band, Tassel, Cockade & Triangular Wood box. 4/16/6. To, 'Brilliant' Frigate, Great Yarmouth to the care of Rev Thos Baker.

BLACKWOOD Capt Henry: 2 Mar 1799. George's Inn. Full Navy Hat, Gold Lace & 2 Wood boxes. 4/14/6; Frock Navy Hat & Trimmings, 2/15/0.

BLACKWOOD Capt (Hy): Navy.27 May/17 Dec 1802: Folding Hat, 2/2/0. Masehurst Lodge, Sussex.// Round Hat 7¼ & Wood box, 1/8/0. 8.117

BLACKWOOD Capt Henry: Navy. 23 Feb 1803. Round Hat 7¼, Crepe Band, 1/9/0.

BLACKWOOD Capt Henry: 6 Jan 1806. Gold Lace & Crepe Band. This order was placed just 3 days before Blackwood acted as the Train

Bearer to Admiral Sir Peter Parker at Nelson's funeral on the 9th January 1806.

References

(1) Williams Sir. E. DICTIONARY OF NATIONAL BIOGRAPHY. The Compact Edition. London: Oxford University Press, 1975. Vol 1. p167

(2) Clowes, W.L. THE ROYAL NAVY. A History from the Earliest Times to 1900. London: Chatham Publishing 1997. Vol 4. pp216-26 (Clowes)

(3) Clowes, Vol 4. pp420-2

(4) Nicolas, Sir. N. THE DISPATCHES AND LETTERS OF LORD NELSON. The Nicolas Edition. London: Chatham Publishing, 1998. Vol IV p143-4

(5) Oman, Carola. NELSON. London: The Reprint Society by arrangement with Hodder & Stoughton, 1950. pp515-6.

(6) Nicolas, V11. p226

(7) Nicolas, V11. p96

(8) Nicolas V11. p cxcv

(9) Nicolas, Vol 1V. p454

(10) Pocock, T. HORATIO NELSON. Chatham: Pimlico Edition, Mackays, 1994. p313

CAPTAIN HON THOMAS BLADEN CAPEL

Captain Thomas Bladen Capel (Capel) was born on the 25th August 1776. He was the youngest son of the 4th Earl of Essex. (Members of his family were already regular customers at Mr Lock's Shop). Whilst some of his elder brothers were to serve in the Army, Capel was destined for the Navy. His name was entered on the books of the 38 Gun Frigate HMS Phaeton on the 22nd March 1782 as a Captain's Servant. (He was then aged only 6 years but this was not an uncommon practise in the Navy at this time). However, in 1792 he is recorded as having joined the 80 Gun Ship HMS Sans Pariel as a 16-year-old Midshipman. (1).

The Sans Pariel was on the Newfoundland Station and then returned to the Home Station. Capel was to remain in the Sans Pariel and on the 23rd July 1795 was present at the action off Groix with Rear-Admiral Lord Hugh Seymour's Fleet. (2) After 5 years service as a Midshipman, he was promoted on the 5th April 1797 to Lieutenant and posted to the 40 Gun Frigate HMS Cambrian on the Home Station. His first contact with Nelson came on the 11th April 1798. He was posted as a Lieutenant to the 74 Gun Ship HMS Vanguard, Nelson's Flagship in the Mediterranean.

Capel became Nelson's Flag Lieutenant on Vanguard and on the 1st August 1798 was present at the Battle of the Nile. (3) On the 5th August 1798 a copy of Nelson's dispatches were given to Capt Berry, Nelson's Flag Captain, to take to Admiral Lord St Vincent. He departed in HMS Leander but was captured with the dispatches by the French on the 18th Aug 1798 and later released. To replace Captain Berry on Vanguard, Capt Thomas Hardy was moved from the 18 Gun Brig HMS Mutine. Capel was then promoted to Commander and took charge of the Mutine. He was despatched on the 13th August 1798 with a duplicate set of Nelson's dispatches for London.

He travelled first by sea to Naples then overland through Europe via Vienna and thence to London.

Capel arrived at Naples on 4th September 1798. The news of Nelson's victory over the French Fleet was received with "rapture". The King of the Two Sicilies, the Queen, Lady Hamilton and the population were ecstatic. Capel and Lieutenant Hoste (also from the Mutine) were feted and driven round Naples in a carriage accompanied by Lady Hamilton. In a letter to Nelson dated 4th September 1798, Capel recorded their arrival in Naples where they were met with applause and acclamation, the Queen and Lady Hamilton both fainted, and he (Nelson) was proclaimed the "...Saviour of Europe". (4)

Capel departed overland from Naples for Vienna, which he reached on the 19th September 1798 and was gained feted. He eventually reached London on the 2nd October 1798. Here, as in Naples and Vienna, the news was received with great rejoicing and relief. He was promoted to Post Captain on the 27th December 1798 and appointed on the 5th January 1799 to the 20 Gun Frigate HMS Arab on the West Indies Station. Here he transferred to the 32 Gun Frigate HMS Meleager. On the 9th June 1801 the Meleager was wrecked on the Triangles in the Gulf of Mexico. However, all the crew were rescued and Capel returned home. (5)

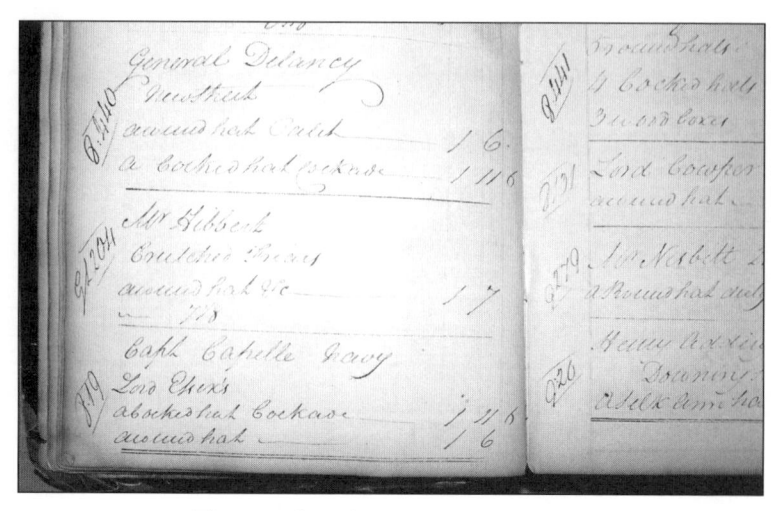

Figure 6: Capt Capel's Order Sept 1802.

Capel was appointed to the command of the 32 Gun Frigate HMS Phoebe. He joined Captain Blackwood's Squadron in the Mediterranean in 1802. This squadron was under Nelson's command and carried out the task of searching for and reporting any movements of the French Fleet. He remained with the squadron and on the 19th October 1805 noted the preparations for departure of the enemy fleet in Cadiz Harbour. These reports were passed to Nelson's Flagship the 100 Gun HMS Victory. The Frigate squadron then received their orders on the 21st October 1805 as to their role in the forthcoming battle. Following the battle Capel in Phoebe played a vital role in salvaging "Prize Vessels". Vice-Admiral Collingwood, who took over command after Nelson's death, recorded Capel's work in his dispatches: He wrote about the outstanding work Capel did to save the French Swiftsure and with Capt Malcolm, the Bahama.

Post Trafalgar

Capel returned home and sat on the Court Martial of Vice-Admiral Sir Robert Calder. On the 27th December 1805 he was appointed to the 40 Gun Frigate HMS Endymion and missed Nelson's funeral. He sailed on a special mission carrying Mr Arbuthnot the English Ambassador to Turkey. There were at this time problems in the relationship between Turkey and England fostered by the French. Turkey threatened and in fact blockaded the Dardanelle's. His trip was eventful, not least in the fact that Mr Arbuthnot was not able to negotiate directly with the Turkish government and then fell ill. An English Squadron under vice Admiral Sir J Duckworth was sent to add weight to negotiations but failed to make any real impression and the squadron and Capel withdrew.

Capel was then posted to the North American Station and made a CB in 1815. In 1821 he was appointed to the Royal Yacht serving until 27 May 1825, when he was appointed Rear Admiral. In 1832 he was appointed a KCB and on the 30th May 1834 was appointed C in C East Indies & China and served until January 1837. He was appointed Vice-Admiral on the 10th January 1837 and returned to England. He was appointed Admiral on the 28th April 1847.

In 1847 Capel was involved with other senior naval officers in trying to decide which Naval Actions should be recognised for the award of medals to those who had survived. The London Gazette noted the establishment of a Board for this purpose. Prior to this time only selected officers were given medals by command of the King. (During the period 1790-1815 this was George 111). Trafalgar was such an action and the King awarded Gold Medals to all the Captains. However, medals could and had been given by individual public figures. Alexander Davison, Nelson's friend and prize agent, gave medals at his own expense to all those who took part with Nelson at the Battle of the Nile. This however was the exception.

Thus the task that Capel and his colleagues (Admiral Byam Martin; Rear- Admiral Gordon; and Admiral Gage) had been given proved to be difficult and somewhat unsatisfactory. The period for debate was extended on the 7th June 1848. Eventually a list of actions was prepared for awards, and medals were ready for issue by 25th January 1849. (6) On the 13th September 1848 Capel was appointed C in C Portsmouth a post he relinquished in September 1851. He died on the 4th March 1853.

Nelson's Correspondence

Nelson had an ambivalent attitude towards Capel. In a letter dated 10 Apr 1799 to Capt Berry he rebukes Capel for not having written to him. (7) This was perhaps a lack of knowledge on Nelson's part as Capel had been posted to the West Indies. He was however, again in Nelson's "bad books" following an action in the Mediterranean in 1803. Nelson wrote to Sir Alexander Ball (a colleague in Malta) on the 13 Aug 1803 about some escape that Capel had been fortunate in, suggesting it was more than he deserved, "… but he is a good young man". (8)

Nelson, despite his criticism obviously respected Capel for he placed a relative of Lady Hamilton's in HMS Phoebe. This was Midshipman Charles Connor. Nelson wrote to Lady Hamilton on 26 Aug 1803 that Connor was getting on very well with Capt Capel. (9) However, Nelson later wrote to Lady Hamilton on the 27 May 1804 saying that he had transferred Connor to the Victory as he felt Capel was too lenient with the Midshipmen. (10) Connors was however mentally ill and Nelson had him transferred him to HMS Niger and returned to Plymouth in March 1805, bound. (11)

Hats from Lock & Co

CAPEL Thos Bladen (Midshipman): 15 Sept 1794. At Lord Essex. Round Hat 7¼, 1/3/0.

CAPEL Captain Hon Thomas Bladen: Navy. 12 Nov 1801. At Lord

Essex. Cockt Hat & Cockade, 1/11/6; Cockt Hat, 1/6/0.

CAPEL Capt Hon Thomas Bladen: Navy. 6 Sept 1802. At Lord Essex's. Round Hat, 1/6/0; Cockt Hat & Cockade, 1/14/0.

CAPEL Capt (Hon Bladen) Navy: 27/28 Sept 1808. Round Hat 7 Full, 1/13/-:// Glazed Hat 7 Full.

CAPEL Hon B, Navy: 31 May 1809. Round Hat 7 Full, 1/13/0.

CAPEL Capt Hon B: 12 Feb 1812. Hat Drest.

References

(1) Williams, Sir. E. DICTIONARY OF NATIONAL BIOGRAPHY. The Compact Edition. London: Oxford University Press, 1975. Vol 1. p308
(2) Clowes, W. L. THE ROYAL NAVY. A History from the Earliest Times to 1900. London: Chatham Publishing, 1997. Vol 4. p260 (Clowes)
(3) Nicolas, Sir N. THE DISPATHCES AND LETTERS OF LORD NELSON. The Nicolas Edition. London: Chatham Publishing, 1998. Vol 111. p8 (Nicolas)
(4) Nicolas, Vol 111. p71
(5) Clowes, Vol 4. p551
(6) Clowes, Vol 6. p213
(7) Nicolas Vol 111. p320
(8) Nicolas, Vol V. p162
(9) Nicolas Vol V11. p379.
(10) Nicolas, V1. p36.
(11) Oman, C. NELSON. London: Reprint Society, Hodder & Staughton Ltd, 1950. p476.

CAPTAIN HENRY DIGBY

Captain Henry Digby (Digby) was the eldest son of the Rev Hon William Digby, Dean of Durham. He was born at Bath 20th Jan 1770 and entered the Royal Navy in 1783 under Rear-Admiral Alexander Innes in the West Indies. He served for 6 years on various stations that included: West Indies; Newfoundland; and the North Sea. In October 1790 he passed his Lieutenant's exams, and then served under Capt Hon Seymour Finch on the 64 Gun Ship HMS Lion in the West Indies. He remained here until the early part of 1795 when he returned to England and was appointed Commander. He joined the 14 Gun Fireship HMS Incendiary and was present at the action off Groix on the 23rd June 1795. He was promoted 'Captain' on the 19th December 1796. In 1797 he joined the Mediterranean Fleet under Lord St Vincent as Captain of the 28 Gun Frigate HMS Aurora. (1)

In the Mediterranean his task was to harass the French shipping in the area off the west coast of Spain and Bay of Biscay. He distinguished himself capturing French merchant ships and privateers. On the 22nd June 1798 he destroyed the French 20 Gun Ship Egalite in the Bay of Biscay. (2) He transferred to the 74 Gun Ship HMS Leviathan as Flag Captain to Commodore Duckworth. A squadron of ships under Duckworth was detached by St Vincent to take on board troops and take the Island of Minorca from the Spanish.

On the 7th November 1798 the squadron arrived off the port of Fornello. Troops were landed under General Hon Charles Stuart's command and met little resistance. Over the next 8 days Stuart's forces supported by Duckworth's squadron moved through the island. On the 15th Nov 1798 the Spanish forces surrendered. (3) Digby remained in Leviathan and in the spring of 1799 reinforced Nelson's squadron and sailed on the 13th June 1799 for Palermo where the King of The Two Sicilies currently had his court. (The King had fled, with the help of Nelson, following the earlier successful attack of the French forces on Naples. Now he was waiting to return after the French had retreated). Nelson sailed with his reinforced squadron from Palermo and arrived off Naples on the 24th June 1799.

Digby then moved from Leviathan to take command of the 32 Gun Frigate HMS Alcmene and cruised off the Spanish coast. During the period 17th–18th October 1799, Captain Digby was part of a small flotilla of Frigates that captured two Spanish Frigates off the West Coast of Spain. These were the 34 Gun Frigates Thetis and Santa Brigida. The Thetis was eventually captured off the Ferrol and the Santa Brigida off Cape Finistere. Both were found to be carrying considerable treasure and became prizes of the British Frigates. The two Spanish frigates were taken to Plymouth and their treasure unloaded. Captain Digby's share of the prize money amounted to over £40,000. By the age of 30 years Digby was estimated to have earned over £51,000 in prize money and by 1804 a further £7000. (4)

In late 1800 Digby was involved in the preparations for the attack on Holland through Copenhagen. A Fleet under the command of Admiral Sir Hyde Parker was assembled at Yarmouth (Norfolk) and included a squadron of ships under Nelson. Digby commanded the 18 Gun Brig HMS Kite. This small fast vessel was used to take dispatches to and from Hyde Parker to the Admiralty in London. In addition Digby took officials and officers concerned with negotiations between the Dutch and British governments prior to and after the hostilities.

Negotiations failed and on the 2nd April 1801 an action, referred to as the Battle of Copenhagen took place. Following this battle a negotiated Peace Treaty was agreed. Digby continued to take dispatches and personnel between England and Holland. On the 19th

June 1801 Nelson resigned his command and sailed for England in the Kite. He arrived at Great Yarmouth on the 1st July 1801. (5)

Digby does not appear to have taken part in any notable actions until his appointment to the 64 Gun Ship HMS Africa. He was ordered to reinforce Nelson's Fleet off Cadiz and joined it on the 14th October 1805. During the period 19th-20th October 1805 the Franco-Spanish Fleet prepared for action and sailed from Cadiz Harbour. Nelson had received this news and dined with his captains on the 20th October 1805. During the night of the 20th October 1805 Captain Digby's ship fell behind Nelson's Fleet. On the morning of the 21st October 1805 Digby was some 6 miles adrift of the fleet. He made haste and caught up with Nelson's Fleet about the same time as the action commenced. However, he mistook a signal made to the fleet from Nelson's Flagship Victory. As a result he passed down part of the Franco-Spanish Fleet and gave each ship in turn a broadside from his guns.

Digby then came alongside the 140 Gun Spanish Ship Santissma Trinidad that had already been in action against several other British ships. Digby engaged this ship despite the fact Africa was one of the smallest ships in Nelson's Fleet. Digby received no response from the Spanish ship and thought that she had struck her flag. He thus sent over a boarding party to take her as a prize. When the boarding party arrived they were firmly told the ship had not surrendered and asked the British crew to leave, which they did. Digby then sighted another enemy ship, the 74 Gun French L'Intrepide. He caught up with and engaged her.

There followed an action that lasted for nearly an hour and fortunately at this time the 74 Gun Ship HMS Orion commanded by Captain Codrington came to help the Africa. She was by then seriously damaged and most of her guns out of action. The L'Intrepide struck her flag to the Orion. Digby and his crew could now count the cost of the action. Africa had heavy damage to masts and rigging and hull: her crew had also suffered considerably with 18 killed and 44 wounded, a total of 62 out of a crew of about 490. (6)

In a report on the part played by Digby and his crew, it stated: ".... that Captain Digby had voluntarily engaged so superior a force...the Africa had performed as gallant a part as any ship of the British Line". Admiral Collingwood, in his Public Testimony, included Captain Digby's name. Digby received the thanks of both Houses of Parliament, a sword, and Gold Medal from His Majesty King George 111. On 17th March 1806 Digby married Lady Jane Elizabeth Andover, the widow of Charles Viscount of Andover. She was the eldest daughter of T W Coke of Holkham Hall, Norfolk. Digby and Lady Andover (she kept this title) had two sons and one daughter. They lived at Minterne Magna, Dorset and had a London residence at 78 Harley Street.

Digby continued to serve in the navy and in 1815 was subjected to some very unpleasant insinuations about his conduct at the Battle of Trafalgar. Digby sought help from Captain Sir Thomas Hardy who was Nelson's Captain at the time of Trafalgar. Hardy wrote to Captain Digby: "I try to assure you that Lord Nelson expressed great satisfaction at the gallant manner in which you passed through the enemy's line; and I assure you he appeared fully satisfied with the conduct of the Africa". Hardy assured Digby that he would personally be happy to contradict the report if he, Digby, passed him the name of the person concerned. (7)

In 1815 Digby was appointed CB and raised to KCB in 1831. On the 12th August 1819 Digby was promoted to Rear-Admiral and on the 22nd July 1830 to Vice-Admiral. He was appointed C in C Nore (Sheerness) on 27th July 1840 and made Admiral on 23rd November 1841 when he retired. (8) He died at his home in Dorset on the 18th September 1842. A brass Plaque was erected in St Andrew's Church,

Minterne Magna commemorating his life.

Nelson Correspondence

There are no letters between Digby and Nelson to be found in Nicolas's Letters and Dispatches. Digby is mentioned in some letters about Nelson's Claim for Prize Money against Lord St Vincent. (9), (10)

Hats from Lock & Co

DIGBY Capt (Sir) Henry: 25 Nov 1799. 35 St James's St. Cockt Hat 7¼ Bare & Cockade, 1/11/6.
This was probably just after he had returned to Plymouth with the two Spanish Frigates and their treasure.

DIGBY Capt (Sir Henry): 14 June 1800: Morris's Hotel. Cockt Hat 7¹/₈, Cockade & Lining, 1/14/0.
This visit was in the summer of 1800 when he was on shore. Currently no further records have been found of any visits to Locks after 1800. (Digby's father in law, TW Coke, was a very regular customer and one of sons, Edward, was to give his name to the Coke Hat, the shape and style more commonly known as known as a Bowler. (The Coke is still made for Lock & Co).

References

(1) Ralfe, J. THE NAVAL BIOGRAPHY OF GREAT BRITIAN. London: Whitmore & Fenn, 1828. Vol 1V. pp 128-32
(2) Clowes, W.L. THE ROYAL NAVY. A History from the Earliest Times to 1900. London: Chatham Publishing, 1997. Vol, 4. p555 (Clowes)
(3) Clowes, Vol 4. pp377-8
(4) Clowes, Vol 4. pp525-6
(5) Nicolas, Sir. N. THE LETTERS AND DISPATCHES OF LORD NELSON:

THE NICOLAS EDITION. London. Chatham Publishing, 1998. Vol 4. pp420-1 (Nicolas)

(6) Nicolas, Vol VII. pp188-9 &192-3

(7) Marshall, J. ROYAL NAVY BIOGRAPHY. London: Longman Hurst Orme & Brown. 1823-35. Vol 1, Part ii. pp762-4.

(8) Clowes, Vol 6. p224

(9) Nicolas, Vol V. p308

(10) Nicolas, Vol V. p370

CAPTAIN RICHARD KING

Captain Richard King (King) was born on the 28th November 1774 the only son of Admiral Sir Richard King Bt. His father was a distinguished Naval Officer and a regular customer at Lock's. King entered the navy in 1788 as a Midshipman in HMS Crown under the command of Commodore William Cornwallis (Cornwallis) on the East Indies Station. He remained with Cornwallis from 1788 to 1794. (1) During that time he was promoted Lieutenant in 1791, Commander in 1793 and Captain on the 14th May 1794. (2)

King retuned to England in November 1794 and was appointed Captain of the 28 Gun Frigate HMS Aurora. He then served in this ship and other Frigates from 1794 to 1804. He was to take part in several actions with the Channel Fleet and two are of interest.

On the 24th October 1798 whilst patrolling in the North Sea in the 44 Gun Frigate HMS Sirius King fought an action against two Dutch Frigates off Texel. These were the 36 Gun Furie and the 26 Gun Waakzaamheid. The two Dutch Frigates were some distant apart and King managed to isolate the Furie which surrendered after the first shot fired by the Sirius. King put a "prize crew" on this vessel and then pursued the Waakzaamheid. This ship had not come to the aid of the Furie. After a sharp action it too "struck". The Royal Navy purchased both vessels. (3)

On the 26th January 1801 King in the Sirius was part of a squadron of Frigates that intercepted the French 36 Gun Frigate Dedaigneuse making for the Port of Rochefort. A long chase followed and eventually on the night of the 27th-28th January 1801 the Sirius and the 36 Gun Frigate HMS Oiseau brought the French ship to action, and the French Captain surrendered. The Royal Navy bought the Dedaigneuse. (4)

In 1804 King was appointed Captain of the 74 Gun Ship HMS Achille and sailed to join Vice-Admiral Cuthbert Collingwood's small force watching for the French Fleet off Cadiz. On The 26th August 1805 Vice-Admiral Villeneuve's Fleet drove this small force off its station as it entered Cadiz, some Spanish Ships of the Line followed. Collingwood's Fleet returned and was reinforced by another 74 Gun Ship HMS Mars. In the resulting action at Trafalgar on the 21st of October 1805, King and his crew in the Achille were heavily involved against the enemy line. (5)

King was in Collingwood's Squadron that broke through the rear line of the Franco-Spanish Fleet about midday on the 21st October 1805. King engaged the Spanish 74 Gun Ship Montanez. This ship sheered off and King saw that HMS Belleisle (Captain Hargood) was heavily pressed. He attempted to reach her but was blocked by the 80 Gun Spanish Ship Arganauta. King engaged and caused her considerable damage and casualties. King thought that she had surrendered but as he attempted to prepare a prize crew two French ships attacked him. The French Ship Achille sailed past and opened fire but did not stop. The second ship the 74 Gun Berwick engaged King's ship. The action was intense but the Berwick struck, and a prize crew was put on board both her and the Arganauta, now wallowing astern. Achilles' log recorded: "At quarter past 4 made sail to the Southward, prizes in company....". King's ship was badly damaged but her casualties were comparatively light compared to the two enemy ships. His crew suffered 13 killed and 59 wounded: Total 72. In the Berwick King's prize crew counted 51 bodies including the Captain's and many wounded. The Arganauta was estimated to have suffered 400 casualties. (6)

Post Trafalgar

King continued his service in the Achille under Collingwood. He received: a Gold medal; a sword and the Thanks of Parliament for his services at the Battle of Trafalgar. On the 24th Sept 1806 as part of the fleet under Commodore Sir Samuel Hood in the Channel he took part in the chase of a small squadron of French Frigates that came out of Port Rochefort. In November 1806 on the death of his father, Admiral Sir Richard King Bt, he succeeded to the Baronetcy. He continued in the Achille and was promoted to Commodore. Between 1808 and 1811 he cruised off the west coasts of Spain and France and was engaged in the blockades of Ferrol and Cadiz. On 1 May 1810 he was briefly engaged in action off the Bay of Naples where he supported the 38 Gun Frigate HMS Spartan in her action against Neapolitan gunboats and Frigates. (7)

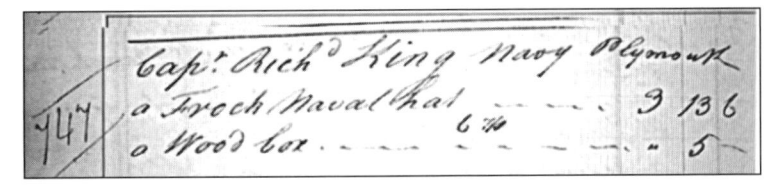

Figure 7: Captain King's Order 1806.

In 1811 he was appointed Captain of the Mediterranean Fleet. On the 12th August 1812 he was promoted Rear-Admiral and raised his flag in the 112 Gun Ship HMS San Josef. He cruised off Toulon and in the Mediterranean uneventfully. On the 2nd Jan 1815 he was appointed KCB and from 1816-1819 was C in C East Indies & China Station, being relieved by Rear-Admiral Sir Henry Blackwood. On his return to England he was appointed a Vice-Admiral on 19th July 1821. On the 23rd July 1833 he was appointed C in C Nore. He was to die from Cholera at Admiralty House, Sheerness on the 5th August 1834. King married twice, both wives being the daughters of his senior commanders. He had children from both marriages, and his second son, by his first marriage, followed him into the Royal Navy and become an Admiral. (8)

Nelson's Correspondence

Currently the author has found no correspondence between King and Nelson.

Hats from Lock & Co

KING Capt R: Navy: 8 Apr/7 Nov1797: Old Hummums, Covent Garden. Bedford Hat & Black Silk Lining, 1/6/0.// Cockt Hat, Cockade & Wood box, 1/11/6. On board His Majesty's Ship Sirius.

KING Capt R: 25 Aug/1 Dec 1798: (Serving on HMS Sirius, Sheerness). Cockt Hat 7¼, 1/9/6. Old Hummums. To Service of the Texel TLB at Mr Paget's Agent Victualler, Yarmouth.// Sett of Naval Trimmings & Gold Lace; Wood box. 3/9/0.

KING Captain R: 30 Apr 1799. Royal Hotel. Round Hat & Patch, 1/6/0.

KING Capt Richard: 14 July 1801. Royal Hotel, Pall Mall. Cockt Hat 6?, 1/11/6.

KING Capt Richard. 18 Mar/24 Dec 1802. HMS Sirius. Plymouth Dock. Full Sett of Navy Trimmings, 3/16/0; Sew on Lace & Wood box. // Folding Hat & Cockade, 2/4/6.

KING Capt Richard: Navy. 8 Jan 1803: Kirkman's Hotel. Sett of Navy Trimmings, 1/1/6.

KING Capt R: Royal Navy. 6 Jan 1804. Plymouth Dock. Round Hat 6⅞ & Wood box, 1/8/0.

KING Capt R: 21,28 Mar 1805. Frock Folding Hat 6¾, 3/13/6.// Wood box, 5/0.

KING Capt Richard: 7 June 1806. Plymouth. Frock Naval Hat 6⅞ & Wood box.

KING Sir Richard: 7 June 1808. Achille. Frock Naval Hat +Trimmings, 6⅞, 3/13/6: Wood box, 5/-: Postage 10p

KING Sir Richard: 20 Apr 1809. George St, Plymouth Dock. Frock Naval Hat +Trimmings 3/13/6: wood Box, 5/-: Pair of Epaulettes, 4/- /-.

KING Capt Sir R: 16 May 1811. (B117). 21 Wigmore Street. Round Livery Hat with Silver Bands.

KING Capt Sir R: 13 June 1812. Round Hat & Wood box, 1/19/0.

KING Sir R: 12 April 1813. Full Uniform Folding Hat, Tassels & Bullion Loops.

KING Sir Richard: 27 Feb 1815. Pall Mall. Round Hat 6⅞; Round Livery Hat.

Sir Richard was, like his father, a very regular customer. The records show the various Ships and Ports that Sir Richard used in his career. They also show the different style of Naval hats that he used as well as the hats for his household staff.

References

(1) Williams, Sir. E. THE DICTIONARY OF NATIONAL BIOGRAPHY. The Compact Edition. London: Oxford University Press, 1975. p1135 (DNB)
(2) Clowes, W.L. THE ROYAL NAVY. A History from the Earliest Times to 1900. London: Chatham Publishing, 1997. Vol 5. p42 (Clowes)
(3) Clowes, Vol 4. pp516-7
(4) Clowes, Vol 4. p536
(5) Clowes, Vol 5. pp121
(6) Nicolas, Sir. N. THE DISPATCHES AND LETTERS OF LORD NELSON. The Nicolas Edition. London: Chatham Publishing, 1998. Vol V11. pp176-7
(7) Clowes, Vol 5. pp453-4
(8) DNB. p1135

CAPTAIN THOMAS MASTERMAN HARDY

Captain Thomas Masterman Hardy (Hardy) was born on the 5 April 1769 at Martinstown in Dorset. He was the sixth child and second son of Joseph Hardy of Portisham in Dorset, whence they moved in 1778 (1) He was sent with his elder brother to Crewkerne Grammar School but had always expressed an interest in the Navy. His early career in the navy started on 30th November 1781 aged 12 years, when he joined Captain Francis Roberts (Roberts) of Burton Bradstock, a family friend, in the 14 Gun Brig HMS Helena. A letter dated 6th March 1782 tells his brother of his voyage in the Helena to Ostend and the chase of a privateer. In 1783 he was in HMS Seaford again with Roberts. (2) Hardy appears to have been on the books of several ships and spending time onshore at school until the age of 21 years. His name appeared on the books of the Guardship HMS Carnatic. It his possible that he spent time in the Merchant Fleet. (3)

In 1790 he joined Capt Alexander Hood in the 38 Gun Frigate HMS Hebe and started his full-time naval career as a Midshipman. Hunt quickly noted Hardy's knowledge of seamanship and sailing and promoted him to Master Mate. In 1792 Hunt with Hardy transferred to the 12 Gun Brig HMS Tisiphone and then in 1793 to the 24 Gun Frigate HMS Amphitrite part of Admiral Hood's Fleet in the Mediterranean. On the 10th November 1793 aged 24 years he was promoted Lieutenant and joined the 32 Gun Frigate HMS Meleager under Captain Charles Tyler. Tyler was serving under Captain Nelson's command in the Mediterranean off Genoa.

Hardy had already gained respect for his seamanship. He could readily appreciate a position and take the necessary steps to meet it. In June 1794 Captain Cockburn was appointed to the command of the Meleager and Hardy remained his Lieutenant. He was to take part in the two actions at Toulon in March and July of 1795 for which he was praised. Cockburn and Hardy transferred in August 1796 to the 38 Gun Frigate HMS Minerve. On 10th December 1796 Nelson, now a Commodore, was ordered by Admiral Sir John Jervis to hoist his Board Pennant in the Minerve then at Gibraltar, and with the 32 Gun Frigate HMS Blanche to make for Porto Ferrajo. During this passage the Minerve with the Blanche were in action against two 40 Gun Spanish Frigates off Carthagena on the afternoon of the 20th December 1796. The Minerve was in action against the Santa Sabina, and the Blanche the Ceres. After short actions both Spanish ships surrendered. 1st Lieutenant Culverhouse with Hardy and a Prize Crew from the Minerve took possession of the Sabina. The Minerve then took the heavily damaged prize in tow.

Later, however, another Spanish Frigate was sighted and the prize was cut loose so that the Minerve could manoeuvre. After a brisk action the Spanish Ship withdrew and Nelson sighted three other ships that were identified as a Spanish ship of the line and two Frigates. The Minerve had to withdraw after engaging the enemy and being seriously damaged. Hardy and Culverhouse steered their prize away from the action, hoisted the English Flag, and were themselves attacked. Their action drew the enemy towards them and helped the Minerve to escape, the Spanish Ships wanting to regain the Sabina. The Sabina was recaptured and the Minerve's prize crew taken but later released. Hardy returned to the Minerve at Gibraltar by Nelson's special request on 10th February 1797 (4)

On the 10th February 1797 Nelson set sail from Gibraltar for Cape St Vincent to join Jervis's Fleet. They were sighted by some Spanish Frigates and pursued. In the course of the chase a seaman fell overboard from the Minerve. Hardy immediately ordered a boat to be lowered and with a crew rowed back to save the seaman. Despite the presence of the pursuing Spanish Fleet, Nelson also turned back and rescued Hardy, the crew and the seaman. Nelson was recorded to have said: "By God, I'll not lose Hardy; back the topsail." (5) On reaching

Jervis's Fleet Nelson transferred his pennant to the 74 Gun Ship HMS London. Hardy remained with Cockburn in the Minerve and was part of Sir John Jervis's Fleet at the Battle of Cape St Vincent on 14th February 1797 being heavily involved. Hardy earned high praise for his Captain and crew. After the action the Minerve took part in the chase of the Spanish 130 Gun Ship Santisima Trinidad but was ordered to stand off and took no action. (6)

On the 29th May 1797 Hardy, now a 1st Lieutenant was in command of a group of boats from the Minereve and the 32 Gun Frigate HMS Lively whose crews cut out and captured the 14 Gun French Corvette Mutine. Hardy, Midshipman Edgar and 13 men were wounded in this action. For his bravery Captain Benjamin Hallowell promoted Hardy to Commander of the captured Mutine. This was by a letter to Hardy dated 29th May 1797. (7) Hardy continued in the Mutine with Jervis's Fleet (now Lord St Vincent) and in May 1798 departed from Lisbon with orders and dispatches from Jervis to Nelson. On 5th June 1798 Hardy met Nelson in his 100 Gun Flagship HMS Vanguard with the news of reinforcements for his fleet. Nelson was ordered to find and destroy the French Fleet in the Mediterranean commanded by Vice Admiral F. P. Brueys. Hardy in the Mutine became a communications officer between Jervis and Nelson, as well as searching for the French Fleet.

On the 1st August 1798 the French Fleet was sighted in Aboukir Bay and during the period 1st to 2nd August 1798, Nelson's Fleet in a major action destroyed all but four of the French Fleet, at what was later called the Battle of the Nile. After the action Nelson transferred Captain Berry (Flag Captain on Vanguard) to the 50 Gun Ship HMS Leander to take his dispatches to Jervis. (The French captured Berry before he could reach Jervis, but later released him). Hardy was transferred from the Mutine to the Vanguard. He was made Captain by Nelson and was confirmed in that rank by letter from the Admiralty on 2nd October 1798. (8)

Hardy now began a close association with Nelson until the latter's death at Trafalgar. Nelson sailed for Naples after the Battle of the Nile in Vanguard seriously ill from fatigue and a head wound. Hardy remained in the Mediterranean with Nelson serving at Naples and Sicily. He was concerned about and disapproved of Nelson's close associations with the Court at Naples and Lady Hamilton. However, he did not refuse a Gold Box from the King of Naples for "Services" during that period. On the 8th June 1799 Nelson and Hardy transferred to the 80 Gun Ship HMS Foudryant. On the 13th October 1799 Captain Berry returned to renew his post as Captain to Nelson. Hardy was transferred by Nelson to the 100 Gun Ship HMS Princess Charlotte and ordered to take her to England for major refitting and repairs. He arrived in late December at Plymouth and spent time ashore visiting friends in Dorset and London. He went to meet Lady Nelson and renew acquaintances and became her firm ally. Hardy was to join Nelson again in November 1800 as his Captain. Nelson specifically asked that Hardy should be his Captain. (9)

Hardy was appointed to a succession of ships including the 90 Gun Ship HMS Namur, then the 112 Gun Ship HMS San Josef at Plymouth Dockyard. (This was one of the two Spanish Ships Nelson had captured at the Battle of Cape St Vincent). The San Josef was not yet ready for sea action when Nelson arrived at Plymouth on the 17th Jan 1801. The Dockyard was tardy and Hardy was without Admiralty Orders to complete the ship or her movements. Nelson eventually sailed for Portsmouth where he and Hardy transferred to the 98 Gun Ship HMS St George. They then sailed with other naval ships to Yarmouth (Norfolk) to join Admiral Sir Hyde Parker's Fleet bound for the Baltic. The main Fleet sailed from Yarmouth on the 12th March 1801.

On the 29th March 1801 off Copenhagen, Nelson moved from the St George to the 74 Gun Ship HMS Elephant. Hardy was to join him later and on the night of the 1st April 1801 Hardy carried out soundings of the depth of the channel that Nelson was to use the next day in his attack. (10) He returned to the St George and was not present at the action on the 2nd April 1801 (Battle of Copenhagen). (11) However, Nelson returned to the St George on the 2nd April 1801 and then accompanied by Hardy went in his gig to survey the prizes vessels that had been captured. Hardy then accompanied Nelson on his visit to the Palace at Copenhagen to discuss the terms of an Armistice.

He returned to Portsmouth in August 1801 where he first commanded the 8 Gun Bomb Ship HMS Vesuvius and then moved to the 32 Gun Frigate HMS Isis then being refitted. Whilst on board the Isis he wrote to his brother in law on the 7th November 1801 about Nelson, Copenhagen and his gift to him of 100 acres of land on the Bronte Estate. Apparently Nelson had also given him an apartment in the house. (12) In March 1802 Hardy was appointed to take the Duke of Kent to Gibraltar in the Isis. On his return the Isis was paid off.

Hardy then moved to the 32 Gun Frigate HMS Amphion. In 1803 Nelson was appointed to the Command of the Mediterranean and hoisted his Flag in the 100 Gun Ship HMS Victory at Portsmouth on the 18th May 1803. He sailed on the 20th May1803, accompanied by Hardy in the Amphion. Nelson transferred to the Amphion on the 23rd May 1803 off Brest. The Victory followed and on the 30th July 1803, Nelson and Hardy transferred back to her. They then began the long watch for the French Fleet that culminated first in the chase to the West Indies and then in the Battle of Trafalgar.

Hardy's actions at Trafalgar are often best remembered for two events; the witnessing of Nelson's signature to the Codicil of his Will with Captain Henry Blackwood (13); and the desire from the dying Nelson for Hardy to kiss him. (14) After Nelson's fatal wounding Hardy still had to command the Victory. Nelson asked for Hardy on several occasions and at times it was impossible for him to come to his friend. He came as often as possible and was able to tell the dying Nelson at his last meeting of the (Nelson's) brilliant victory. He is then reported to have kissed Nelson's cheek and departed. The hours between Nelsons's fatal injury to his death and Hardy's support for him, are well recorded. Hardy had the task of reporting Nelson's death to Vice Admiral Cuthbert Collingwood. (15)

After Trafalgar

Hardy had the melancholy task of bringing Nelson's body back to England on the Victory. After repairs at Gibraltar the Victory arrived at St Helens (Isle of Wight) on the 4th December 1805. He was present at the opening of the coffin for the purposes of a post-mortem being carried out. He left Spithead in the Victory on the 11th December 1805 for Greenwich. On the 22nd December 1805 Nelson's body left the Victory and was transferred to Commissioner Grey's Yacht for passage to Greenwich Hospital to "Lie in State". (16) Hardy had two further duties to perform for his old friend, namely: being one of the Bearers of The Banner of Emblems at his State Funeral on the 9th January 1806; and taking Nelson's last letter to Lady Hamilton. Nelson had written this on the morning just before the battle and it lay on his desk. Hardy performed this duty and also took the naval coat and white waistcoat, now blood stained, that Nelson wore at Trafalgar. (17) In his Will, Nelson had left Hardy: " all my Telescopes and Sea Glasses, and one hundred pounds in money to be paid three months after my death". (18)

On the 4th February 1806 Hardy was created a Baronet. He received the Thanks of Parliament, a Sword, and as a Captain 1st Class £2389 7s 6d (his share of the Government's Funds to the crews at Trafalgar, and prize money of about £1000). He transferred to the 74 Gun Ship HMS Triumph and sailed to the North American Station (Halifax and Bermuda) commanded by Vice-Admiral Sir George Berkley. On the 17th November 1807 he married Anne Louisa, the Admiral's eldest daughter, aged 19 years at St Paul's Church, Halifax. (Hardy was aged 40 years.) From December 1807 until April 1808 Hardy and his wife were to spend 6 moths off Chesapeake Bay on Blockade Duty in the Triumph. They then sailed to Bermuda and back to England. He was appointed to the Channel Fleet in the summer of 1808 and in April 1809 he returned to Plymouth and joined Vice-Admiral Berkley now C in C Lisbon as his Flag Captain between 1809-12. His wife was to accompany him and also his brother in law Colonel Berkley who was serving in the Peninsular War with Sir Arthur Wellesley, later the Duke of Wellington.

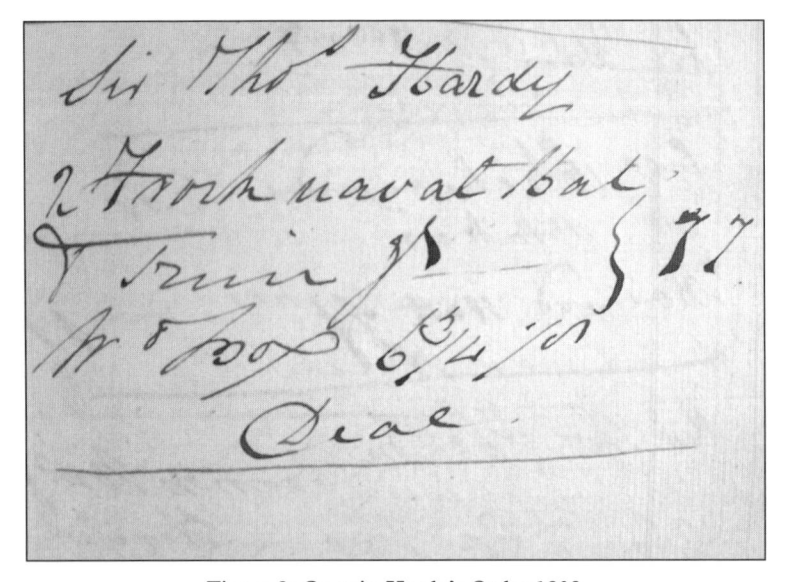

Figure 8: Captain Hardy's Order 1808.

Hardy returned to England in 1812 and in October 1812 was appointed to the 79 Gun Ship HMS Ramilles to command a Squadron on the North American Station as Commodore. On cessation of the 2nd American War under the 1814 Treaty of Ghent, Hardy returned home. On 17th June 1815 he was nominated K.C.B. and from the 23rd June 1815 to 11th August 1819 was Captain of the

Royal Yacht Princess Augusta. He spent some time at the Admiralty between Royal duties working on new designs of armament and ship construction. He first rented a house in London, then moved to Teignmouth and finally to Stonehouse near Plymouth.

In 1816 Hardy had to protect his young wife from libellous statements about her behaviour. To this end he obtained £1000 in damages from the Morning Herald; and was to fight a duel with Lord Buckingham over this matter. Lord March acted as Hardy's Second and though shots were fired no injuries occurred. The matter was subsequently resolved. On the 12th August 1819 Hardy was appointed Commodore and C in C South American Station, and sailed on the 19th September 1819 with his pennant in the 74 Gun Ship HMS Superb. He had been chosen especially for the post that required tact and firm control. He had to guard British Trade and ensure safe passage of British vessels free from American Privateers. In 1820 he was appointed Colonel of Marines. Hardy returned to England in January 1824 in HMS Creole.

During his absence, at his suggestion, Lady Hardy had travelled round Europe with their family. Hardy, after a stay in London, joined his family abroad. (19) On the 27th May 1825 Hardy was appointed Rear-Admiral some twenty years after The Battle of Trafalgar. He visited Paris in June/July 1825 where he met Wellington. In 1826 he was appointed Chairman of the Government Committee on Marine Construction. In December 1826 he was ordered to take a force to Lisbon where there was unrest. He sailed in the 74 Gun Ship HMS Wellesley escorting a convoy and returned in the early part of 1827. He then bought the Riccard Estate near Portisham in Dorset where his family had been tenant farmers. On the 21st October 1827 he Struck his Flag never to return to a sea command.

During 1828 Hardy quietly got on with his work at the Admiralty and enjoying his family. He took a house in Brighton and commuted to

London. His daughters were presented at King George 111's Court on 4th May 1829. On the death of King George 111, Prince William ascended the throne on the 30 September 1830 as King William 1V. He approved the appointment of Hardy as First Sea Lord in November 1830. This appointment suited Lady Hardy who was a great socialite of the times. (20)

With the change in Government in 1834 Hardy was appointed on the 8th April 1834 Governor of Greenwich Hospital. He kept his appointment as 1st Sea Lord until a successor was found. Hardy travelled to Windsor on the 10th April 1834 to kiss the hand of William 1V to complete the necessary formalities to his new office. In 1835 Hardy was involved in a discussion regarding the "true" origins of Horatia Nelson. Hardy does not seem to have believed Horatia was a result of a union as between Nelson and Lady Hamilton. In the codicil to his Will, (that Hardy had witnessed), Nelson had written in reference to Horatia: "…whom I acknowledge as my adopted daughter." Hardy had in 1812 sought an answer from Lady Hamilton on the question of Horatia's parentage. Her reply in a letter of 1812 received by Hardy on 17th October 1812, stated: My dear Sir Thomas, Let me only say to you that which is true. Horatia is our dear Nelson's daughter. May God bless you! Emma Hamilton." Hardy, even in his old age, was still of the opinion the child was not Nelson's and Lady Hamilton's. (21)

In 1837 he was promoted Vice-Admiral by seniority and elected an Elder Brother of Trinity House. During his tenure at Greenwich he and Lady Hardy were to entertain many friends and dignitaries. Here he presided with his usual tact and wisdom though Lady Hardy spent much of her time in London Society. Hardy was taken ill at Greenwich on 13th September 1839 and died on the 20th September 1839. He was buried in a Mausoleum in the Hospital Cemetery. Having no sons (3 daughters) the Baronetcy became extinct. Lady Hardy's widowhood lasted just over one year and she then married

Lord Seaford. (22)

Nelson Correspondence

Much of the correspondence between Nelson and Hardy refers to naval matters. There are letters indicating the actions Hardy was to take and memoranda to the same effect when he was Flag Captain to Nelson. There are however some letters from Nelson to prominent people that show his great regard for Hardy. Nelson wrote to Sir John Jervis on the 20th December 1796 off Carthagena and referred to the actions of certain naval lieutenants: "Lieutenants Hardy, Gage, and Noble, deserve every praise which gallantry and zeal justly entitle them to..." (23)

In 1799 Nelson transferred Hardy to HMS Princess Charlotte and ordered him to England with letters and dispatches. In a personal letter to Evan Nepean (Secretary to the Admiralty) from Palermo dated 9th November 1799 Nelson recommended Hardy to the members of the Admiralty Board in the strongest terms. (24)

In August 1805 Hardy's health had deteriorated and Nelson persuaded him to see the Ship's Surgeon. Hardy obtained a letter from the Victory's surgeon that recommended he be permitted to go ashore to recuperate. Nelson sought approval for this matter from the Admiralty, enclosing Hardy's letter and one from the Fleet' Physcian. Nelson wrote on the 18th August 1805 from the Victory off Spithead to William Marsden, Secretary at the Admiralty to indicate Hardy's deterioration in health and "..the necessity of his being permitted to go ashore for a short time, for the recovery thereof". The request was granted retrospectively, Nelson having put Hardy ashore to recuperate at Gibraltar. Hardy returned to the Victory in September 1805. (25)

Hats from Lock & Co

Hardy was not a customer until after the Battle of Trafalgar. He called in at Locks in June 1808 and his order reads:

HARDY Sir Thomas: 9 June 1808. 2 Frock Naval Hats and Trimmings, (Size) 6¾. 7/7/-: Wood box. To Deal.
This order was placed soon after he had returned from Bermuda with his young wife. The order shows that though he was stated to be a well-built man, his hat size was just above average for the period 1790-1815. (By comparison Nelson's hat size was 7 to 7/¼.) Hardy was at this time appointed to the Channel Fleet, that may account for the address-To Deal.

References

(1) Gore, J. NELSON'S HARDY AND HIS WIFE. London: John Murray, 1935. p4 (Gore)
(2) Gore p5
(3) Gore p6
(4) Nicolas, Sir N.H. THE DISPATCHES AND LETTERS OF LORD NELSON; THE NICOLAS EDITION: London: Chatham Publishing, 1997. Vol II. p331 (Nicolas)
(5) Gore p12.
(6) Clowes, W.L. THE ROYAL NAVY. A History from the Earliest Times to 1900. London: Chatham Publishing, 1997. Vol 4. pp318-9 (Clowes)
(7) Gore. p13.
(8) Nicolas, Vol. III p 56
(9) Pope, D. THE GREAT GAMBLE: Nelson at Copenhagen. London: Weidenfeld & Nicolson, 1972. p86 (Pope)
(10) Clowes, Vol 4. p432
(11) Pope. p455
(12) Gore. p25.
(13) Clowes, Vol 5. p135

(14) Clowes, Vol 5. p145.
(15) Nicolas, Vol VII. pp244-51
(16) Nicolas, Vol VII. p309
(17) Munday J. in White C.D. (Ed) THE NELSON COMPANION. Stroud: Royal Naval Museum Publications & Sutton Publishing Ltd, 1997. pp68-9
(18) Nicolas, Vol VII. ccxxi.
(19) Gore. p12
(20) Gore. p147
(21) Nicolas, Vol VII. p386
(22) Gore. p200
(23) Nicolas, Vol II. p313
(24) Nicolas, Vol IV. p94
(25) Nicolas, VII. pp11-12

CAPTAIN THOMAS FRANCIS FREMANTLE

Captain Thomas Francis Fremantle (Fremantle) was born on the 20th November 1765. He was the third son of John Fremantle of Aston Barton in Buckinghamshire and entered the Royal Navy in 1777 aged 12 years. His first ship was the 36 Gun Frigate HMS Hussar under Captain Francis Reynolds watching the Portuguese Coast. In 1779 he transferred to the Jamaica Station under Capt Sir Hyde Parker (Hyde Parker) and served in the 50 Gun Ship HMS Jupiter, then the 44 Gun Frigate HMS Phoenix. (1) On the 4th October 1780 Phoenix was wrecked in a hurricane off the coast of Cuba but he and the crew survived. (2)

Fremantle remained on the Jamaica Station for a further 7 years serving in various ships. He was promoted by Hyde Parker to Lieutenant on 13th March 1783 and returned to England in December 1787. In 1790 at the time of Spanish re-armament, Fremantle again served under Hyde Parker now in the 74 Gun Ship HMS Brunswick. He was promoted Commander on 30th November 1790. In 1791 he was given command firstly of the 16 Gun Sloop HMS Spitfire then the 14 Gun Incendiary Fire-ship Conflagration. On the 16th May 1793 he was appointed Post Captain and transferred to the 28 Gun Frigate HMS Tartar and joined Vice-Admiral Lord Samuel Hood's Fleet (Hood) in the Mediterranean. (3)

On the 27th August 1793 he led Hood's Fleet into Toulon Harbour, in which Nelson was also serving. He and Fremantle were to become firm friends. Nelson soon came to appreciate Fremantle's professional abilities and courage. Fremantle then served under Nelson in his detached squadron in the Mediterranean, authorised by Hood. In 1794 he was engaged again in Tartar with Nelson at the siege of Bastia, shelling the port.

On the 13 March 1795, now in the 36 Gun Frigate HMS Inconstant in Vice-Admiral Hotham's Fleet (Hotham), he was present at the action off Toulon and took a major initial role in the capture of the French 80 Gun Ship Ca-Ira. This ship had been partially disabled through a collision with another French Ship of the Line. Fremantle who was ahead of the main British Fleet saw the opportunity to inflict further damage. He took this and caused many casualties in the Ca-Ira due to the superb seamanship and gunnery of the crew. However, his ship was to come under heavy fire from the Ca-Ira and he was obliged to retire out of range. His crew suffered 3 killed and 14 wounded. (4) The second vessel to reach the Ca-Ira was the 64 Gun Ship HMS Agamemnon, Nelson's Flagship. Nelson recorded the details of the chase and action by Fremantle in his ship's log. He wrote: "…so true did she fire her stern-guns, that not a shot missed some part of the ship…". His actions were also recorded in Admiral Hotham's dispatches. (5)

On the 26th August 1795 Fremantle was again in action as part of Nelson's detached squadron off the coast of Genoa. Nelson had been ordered to harass the French Fleet. In an action off Vado in the bays of Alassio and Langueglia ships from his Fleet captured two French Brigs, two five Gun Galleys and five Store Ships. In addition two further ships were destroyed. He was again in action 20th April 1796 at the capture of the 38 Gun French Frigate Unite; and on the 27 June 1796 he played a major role in the evacuation of the British residents from Leghorn.

He and his crew managed to evacuate: the residents; personal property; and 37 Merchant Vessels, some carrying the 200 bullocks and bread rations that had been bought for the Fleet. Fremantle sent a report of the action to Vice-Admiral Sir John Jervis (Jervis) C in C Mediterranean. Jervis forwarded the report to the Admiralty with a covering letter. (6)

Amongst the British evacuees was the Wynne family and their teenage daughters. One of these, Betsy aged 18 years, was to attract Fremantle's attention. In the passage from Leghorn to Naples their attachment grew and in December 1796 they were married in the British Embassy in Naples. Superintending the arrangements was Lady Hamilton. Betsy Fremantle was to accompany her sailor husband in the Inconstant, transferring with him to the 38 Gun Frigate HMS Seahorse on 1 July 1797.

Two days later, 3rd July 1797, Fremantle was to accompany Nelson in his barge at the action off Cadiz. The town was shelled by the Bomb Ship Thunderer which itself came under heavy fire. Nelson ordered it to withdraw, pursued by Spanish gunboats and launches. Nelson then ordered the British launches and barges to intervene. The resulting action was recorded in Nelson's own short biography: "Sketch of my Life" October 1799. Fremantle was slightly wounded in this action. (7)

In a second action in July 1797 Fremantle and Nelson were severely wounded. Nelson was ordered to attack and seize the town of Santa Cruz on the Island of Tenerife. On the night of the 24th –25th July 1797 the action took place, but went seriously wrong. Nelson was injured by ordnance in his right arm. This required the arm to be amputated above the elbow joint. Fremantle was also wounded in the right arm and this was slow to heal. Nelson retired with his fleet and rendezvoused with Jervis on the 20th August 1797. He transferred his flag from the 74 Gun Ship HMS Theseus to Fremantle's Seahorse. "The wounded Admiral and Captain" were nursed on the journey home by Betsy Fremantle, and arrived in England on the 1st September 1797. (8)

Fremantle had to convalesce, as his wound was slow to heal. He was appointed in August 1800 to the 74 Gun Ship HMS Ganges. He joined Vice-Admiral Sir Hyde Parker's Fleet in January 1801 on the expedition to the Baltic and the attack on Copenhagen. He served in Nelson's squadron in Ganges in the general action on the 2nd April 1801. His crew suffered 5 Seamen killed and 1 Marine wounded. One officer (The Pilot) was also badly wounded. Fremantle accompanied Nelson and Captain Hardy to meet the Dutch Prince Regent following Nelson's offer of a truce. (9)

Shortly after the battle Fremantle was sent on a mission to the Russian Government which at that time was unfavourably disposed to the British, especially the Tsar. The latter however died suddenly and Fremantle's mission was to be successful in representing the friendship of Britain to Russia. Following his service in the Baltic he returned to Jamaica. The resumption of War with France and Spain in 1803 resulted in Fremantle's return to serve in the Channel Fleet in Ganges. In May 1805 he transferred to the 98 Gun Ship HMS Neptune and sailed for the Mediterranean to serve under Nelson.

He was part of Nelson's Weather Column in the action at Trafalgar, and played a major part. He engaged the French 80 Gun Ship Bucentaure causing severe damage and then 100 Gun Spanish Ship Santisma Trinidad. He continued this latter attack until his own ship became unmanageable. His crew suffered a number of casualties: 10 Seamen and one Petty officer killed; 30 Seamen, 3 Marines wounded. (10)

After Trafalgar

After the battle he continued to serve in the Mediterranean under Vice-Admiral Cuthbert Collingwood. In December 1806 he returned to England to take up a post at the Admiralty. He was then appointed to the Yacht William and Mary until 1810 when he was appointed Rear-Admiral on the 31st July 1810. He served for two years in the Mediterranean; and then 2 years in the Adriatic helping the Austrian Army in their defeat of French forces in that region and by May 1814:

"...reduced every remaining French possession in the Adriatic." (11)

Fremantle was to be rewarded for his methodical and careful tactics in the Adriatic with the appointment to KCB on 12th April 1815. He was also to receive a Knighthood (Kt) from the Austrian Government. On the 20th February 1818 he was nominated a GCB and then C in C Mediterranean. He was advanced to Vice-Admiral on the 12 May 1819 and died at Naples on the 19th December 1819. His wife Betsy died on the 2nd Nov 1857. Their eldest son was created a Baron in 1821 and another son was to follow Fremantle into the Royal Navy. He became an Admiral, served in the Crimean War and was C in C Plymouth.

Nelson Correspondence

Two letters are of some note in revealing the attachment Nelson had for Fremantle. As outlined above he had reason to be grateful to Fremantle for his services to him personally; and also to Betsy Fremantle who had nursed him in HMS Seahorse after the loss of his arm at the siege of Santa Cruz on 25th July 1797. The first letter dated Jan 1804 was written whilst Nelson was patrolling the Mediterranean. He detailed to Fremantle his concerns about the various anchorages he had used, decrying Malta as: "..useless: ... I never dare venture to carry the Fleet there. (12)

The second letter is similar in the way Nelson confided to Fremantle his troubles and feelings. In this letter he decried the way one of his colleagues was to be court-martialled for his actions against a Spanish Fleet. He was even more concerned and indignant that his name had been drawn into the affair by holding his exploits up as the standard others should achieve. This was shown in his letter dated 16 Aug 1805 in which he spoke of his grief that people insinuated that Nelson would have done better. He then wished Fremantle to have HMS Neptune close alongside a French three-decker. (13)

Hats from Lock & Co

FREEMANTLE R-Adml Thos: 20 Apr 1814. Round Hat 6¾.

FREEMANTLE Admiral Thos: 20 Apr 1815. Round Hat 6¾

FREEMANTLE Sir Thomas: 16 May 1822. Stone Buildings. Round Hat. A29.

References:

(1) Williams, Sir. E. DICTIONARY OF NATIONAL BIOGRAPHY. The Compact Edition. London: Oxford University Press, 1975. Vol 1. p738

(2) Clowes, W. L. THE ROYAL NAVY. A History from the Earliest Times to 1900. London: Chatham Publishing, 1997. Vol 4. p110 (Clowes)

(3) Clowes, Vol 4. p203

(4) Clowes, Vol 4. pp270-2

(5) Nicolas, Sir N. THE DISPATHCES AND LETTERS OF LORD NELSON. The Nicolas Edition. London: Chatham Publishing, 1998. Nicolas, Vol 11. p13 (Nicolas)

(6) Nicolas, Vol 11. p194

(7) Nicolas, Vol 1. p13

(8) Oman, C. NELSON. Reprint Society, Hodder & Staughton Ltd, 1950. p215-8

(9) Nicolas, Vol 1V p326.

(10) Nicolas, Vol VII. pp186, 222

(11) Clowes, Vol 5. p306

(12) Nicolas, Vol V. p342

(13) Nicolas, Vol V11. p5

CAPTAIN JAMES NICOLL MORRIS

Captain James Nicoll Morris (Morris) was born in 1765. He was the son of Captain James Morris RN who was mortally wounded on the 50 Gun Ship HMS Bristol during the attack on Charlestown on the 28th June 1776 and died on the 2nd July 1776. Morris entered the navy in 1778 aboard HMS Prince of Wales the Flagship of Rear-Admiral Samuel Barrington on the West Indies Station. Morris was present at the engagements at St Lucia and Grenada. He was promoted Lieutenant on the 14 April 1780 in HMS Namur and was present at the action off Dominica 12th January 1782. (1)

In 1790 during the Spanish Re-armament he served in the 98 Gun Ship HMS St George, commanded by Barrington, now a Vice-Admiral. On the 21st September 1790 on the recommendation of Barrington, Morris was promoted to Commander. In 1791 he was appointed into the 20 Gun Sloop HMS Pluto on the Newfoundland Station. On the 25th July 1793 he captured the 20 Gun French Sloop Lutine. Morris was appointed Captain on 7th October 1793 and took command of the 38 Gun Frigate HMS Boston and returned in her to England.

During the next four years Morris served in the Boston in various locations including; The Channel; Bay of Biscay; and off the coast of Spain. He transferred from the Boston to the 38 Gun Frigate HMS Lively in 1797 and was wrecked off Rota Point near Cadiz on 12th April 1798. (2) Morris was rescued and in 1799 was appointed to the 38 Gun Frigate HMS Phaeton. Later in 1799 he was sent on a special mission taking Lord Elgin to Constantinople. He returned from this mission transporting two Turkish Government' Officials. He called at Palermo on the 17th December 1799 where he met Nelson. (3)

Nelson gave him additional orders to be followed after landing the Turkish Officials. He was to find Captain Blackwood in the 32 Gun

Frigate HMS Penelope who was then to come under Morris's command. They were then to patrol off the Capes of Spartel and St Vincent. (4) He carried out the various tasks and in May 1800 was seconded to help the Austrian Army in their action against French Forces retreating to Genoa. (5) He returned to the Spanish Coast and on the 27 October 1800 boats from the Phaeton under Lt Francis Beaufort captured the 14 Gun Spanish Polacco San Josef off the Fortress of Fuengirola near Malaga. In the action one seaman was killed and four wounded. The San Josef was "purchased" for the Navy and renamed HMS Calpe. (6)

Morris continued in the Phaeton and returned to England. In 1802 he transferred to the 50 Gun Ship HMS Leopard and then to the new 74 Gun Ship HMS Colossus. He served in the latter with Admiral Hon William Cornwallis's Channel Fleet watching the French Fleet off the Port of Brest. In August 1805 he was ordered to join Nelson's Fleet in the Mediterranean. He reinforced Vice Admiral Collingwood's "small force" standing off Cadiz. On the 20th August 1805 this force was chased off its station by the arrival of Vice-Admiral Villeneuve's combined fleet that sailed into Cadiz. Collingwood then resumed his watching station. (7)

On the 20th October 1805 Morris, with other captains, was to met with Nelson onboard the Victory (8) Morris remained with Collingwood's squadron, now reinforced, and followed him into action on the 21st October 1805. Morris and his crew were not only to play a substantial part in the action but Morris was to be severely wounded and his crew suffer the most casualties. Colossus's log showed that she was in action from 12-50 when she came under fire. Morris came alongside the French 74 Gun Ship Argonaute, the ships touching. After about 10 minutes firing the French vessel's guns were all but silenced and she fell away.

Whilst the above action was progressing two other enemy ships fired on the Colossus. The French 74 Gun Ship Swiftsure and the Spanish 80 Gun Ship Bahama. The position of the Swiftsure was such as to initially hinder the action of the Bahama. However, as the Swiftsure drifted away badly damaged by Colossus's guns, she exposed the Bahama to one of the Colossus's broadsides of cannon fire. The Bahama surrendered but the Swiftsure again came into action. Morris had seen the Swiftsure's intentions and manouvered so as to engage her with another broadside. By this time the 74 Gun Ship HMS Orion had come to the aid of the Colossus and she too fired a broadside into the Swiftsure. Morris received the surrender of the French ships.

The Colossus was by now severely damaged and unmanageable. Morris had sustained a severe wound to the thigh. He had applied a tourniquet to the injury to try to stem the blood loss and refused to be evacuated from the scene of the action. His crew were to suffer considerable casualties in the actions, 40 were killed and 158 wounded. With the engagement over Morris allowed himself to be taken to his cabin and treated. The Bahama and Swiftsure became prizes of the Colossus; and Morris was eventually landed at Gibraltar where he recovered from his injury. (9)

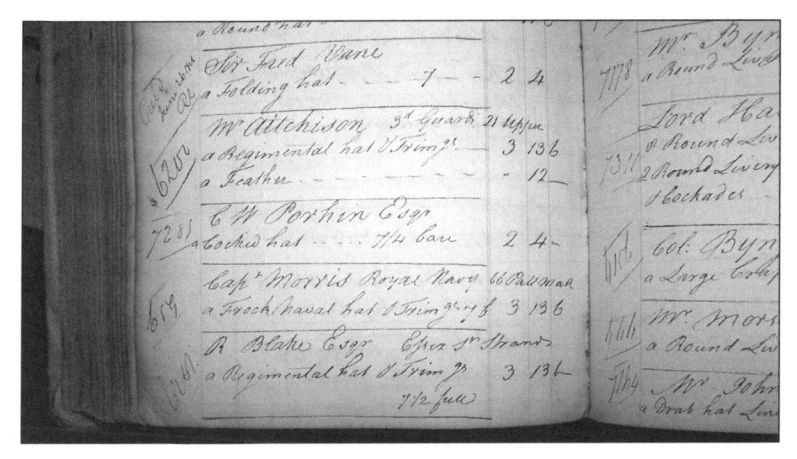

Figure 9: Captain Morris's Order 1806:

Post Trafalgar

Following repairs to the Colossus Morris resumed command, firstly as part of the Home and then the Mediterranean Fleets, the latter with Vice-Admiral Thornborough's Squadron off Toulon, searching for a French Fleet under Rear Admiral Allemand. He returned to England in 1810 and took command of the 98 Gun Ship HMS Formidable. On the 1st August 1811 he was promoted to Rear-Admiral. In 1812, by special request of Vice Admiral Sir James Sumarez, Morris was appointed Third in Command of the Baltic Fleet. On 2nd January 1815 he was nominated KCB and became a Vice–Admiral on the 12 Aug 1819. He died at his home in Harlow on the 15th April 1830.

Nelson Correspondence

Only one letter from Nelson to Morris has been found, outlining the action he has to take. (Nicolas IV p149).

Hats from Lock & Co

MORRIS Capt JN: 20/23 June 1806. Royal Navy. 66 Pall Mall. Frock Naval Hat 7 Bare & Trimmings.// Triangle Wood box, 5/-.

MORRIS Adm (Sir) J: 30 Dec 1811. Park Place. Round Livery Hat & Cockade.

MORRIS Adml J N: 17 Feb 1812. Frock Naval Hat & Trimmings, 3/13/6; 2 Cocked Hats Covered with Oil Silk, Bound & Lynd. Wood box for 2 Hats.

MORRIS Adm J N: 12 Dec 1812. Frock Naval Hat & Trimmings.

MORRIS Adml J N: 21 Aug 1813. Reading. Round Hat.

References

(1) Williams, Sir. E. DICTIONARY OF NATIONAL BIOGRAPHY. The Compact Edition. London: Oxford University Press, 1975. Vol 1. p1426
(2) Clowes, W.L. THE ROYAL NAVY. A History form the Earliest Times to 1900. London: Chatham Publishing, 1997. Vol 4. p549. (Clowes)
(3) Nicolas, Sir N. THE DISPATCHES AND LETTERS OF LORD NELSON. The Nicolas Edition. London: Chatham Publishing, 1997. Vol 1V. p153 (Nicolas)
(4) Nicolas, Vol 1V. p147
(5) Clowes, Vol 4. p416
(6) Clowes, Vol 4. p534
(7) Clowes, Vol 5. p121
(8) Oman Carola. NELSON. London: The Reprint Society by arrangement with Hodder & Stoughton, 1950. p538.
(9) Nicolas, Vol V11. pp174-5

CAPTAIN WILLIAM HARGOOD

Figure 10: Captain Hargood.

Captain William Hargood (Hargood) was born on the 6th May 1762 the youngest son of Hezekiah Hargood a Purser in the Royal Navy (There were nine children in the family). (1) There is a contradictory reference to this statement in which his father is described as: "...an independent gentleman residing on Blackheath in the County of Kent. (2) His name was put on the books of the 74 Gun Ship HMS Triumph on the 27th October 1773 to the 25th Jan 1775. Triumph was the Flagship of Nelson's uncle, Commodore Maurice Suckling, on the Medway Station. However, Hargood did not spend all his time on the Triumph, resuming his studies at school. He joined the 50 Gun Ship HMS Romney under Capt Hon Keith Elphinstone at Deptford on

11th March 1775, part of the Newfoundland Fleet under Rear–Admiral Robert Duff who hoisted his flag in the Romney on 26th May 1775 at Plymouth and with Hargood departed for Newfoundland. On the 27th October 1775 Duff sailed for England and arrived on the 19th November 1775, and struck his flag.

Hargood then joined the 50 Gun Ship HMS Bristol under Commodore Sir Peter Parker, an old friend of the Hargood's father. Hargood was put under Sir Peter's special care. (3) On the 29th Dec 1775 Sir Peter sailed for Cork to pick up a convoy bound for America. He arrived off Cape Fear on 5th April 1776 and anchored off Charleston South Carolina on 4 June 1776. Hargood was present at the attack on Sullivan Island on 28 June 1776 where Sir Peter suffered a head' wound. The Bristol suffered both materially and in casualties with 40 of the crew killed, and Captain Morris of the Bristol lost his right arm.

Hargood continued on the Bristol and was present at the taking of Long Island, New York, on the 14 August 1776. Sir Peter then transferred to the 50 Gun Ship HMS Chatham and sailed for Rhode Island. He captured the island on the 1st December 1776. The Chatham cruised off the American' coast until 22nd July 1777 when Sir Peter was promoted Rear-Admiral and C in C Jamaica. Sir Peter transferred back to the Bristol on 25th December 1777 and sailed on 1st January 1778 for Port Arthur (Jamaica) where he arrived on the 13th February 1778.

On the 20th July 1778 Hargood was to meet Nelson, then a Lieutenant, who joined Bristol as a 3rd Lieutenant from HMS Lowestoft. There friendship started at this time and Nelson remained with Sir Peter becoming 1st Lieutenant in September 1778 and was appointed to the command of the 14 Gun Sloop HMS Badger on 20th December 1778. By coincidence Lieutenant Cuthbert Collingwood (later 2nd in Command at Trafalgar) joined the Bristol as the 1st

Lieutenant on Nelson's departure. He too then took command of the Badger in June 1779.

Hargood remained under Sir Peter's patronage and took part in convoy duties and the seizure of prizes. On the 13th January 1780 aged 18, Hargood received his commission as Lieutenant on the 14 Gun Sloop HMS Port Royal. He sailed for Pensecola where Port Royal provided naval cover for the garrison. He was captured at the "Defence of Pensecola" on 8th May 1781. The garrison was released and sent to New York on the 4th July 1781, from where he returned to England. (4), (5)

Hargood was then appointed in December 1781 as 4th Lieutenant to the 74 Gun Ship HMS Magnificent under Captain Robert Linzee. They sailed for the West Indies on 7th February 1782 and joined Admiral Sir George Rodney's Fleet on the 20th March 1782. Hargood was present at the actions off Dominica on the 9th and 12th April 1782 and capture of the 40 Gun French Frigate L'Aimable on 19th April 1782. On the announcement of "Peace" in 1783, Magnificent returned to England and was "paid off" on 27th June 1783.

Hargood was next commissioned 3rd Lieutenant in the 38 Gun Frigate HMS Hebe on the 23 May 1784, part of the Channel Fleet. In June 1784 Hargood was promoted to 2nd Lieutenant about the same time Prince William (the future King William IV) was appointed as 3rd Lieutenant. He and Hargood were to remain lifelong friends. Such was their friendship that Hargood sough to serve under Prince William. On the 14th April 1786 Prince William was promoted Post Captain to command the Frigate HMS Pegasus. Prince William chose Hargood to be firstly his 2nd then his 1st Lieutenant. In Pegasus they sailed on a visit to the Channel Islands and then to Halifax on the 6th June 1786. They reached Halifax on the 27th June 1786 and then sailed for the West Indies meeting with HMS Boreas under Nelson. Hargood attended the wedding of Nelson to Mrs Fanny Nesbit at which Prince William gave away the bride.

He remained with Prince William and in 1788 moved as his 1st Lieutenant to the 32 Gun Frigate HMS Andromeda. In April 1789 Andromeda was paid off, and in June 1789 Hargood was promoted to Commander. In December 1789 he took command of the Sloop HMS Swallow and was advanced to Post Captain on 22 November 1790. In 1792 Hargood was appointed to command the 24 Gun Frigate HMS Hyaena and sailed for the West Indies. In an action off Cape Tiberon against the French Frigate Concorde of 44 Guns, and two 74 Gun Ships that were closing to join the action, he struck his flag. This was to prevent needless loss of life amongst his crew. He and his crew were captured but Hargood escaped and returned to England where he faced a Court-martial on HMS Cambridge at Hamoaze (Plymouth) for the "Loss of his Ship". He was honourably acquitted on the 11th October 1793.

He then held a number of appointments between 1794-96 including the 32 Gun Frigate HMS Iris. He sailed on convoy duty for Africa on 5 February 1795 and then served with Vice-Admiral Sir Hyde Parker in the Channel Fleet. On 14th Aug 1796 he was appointed to the 50 Gun Ship HMS Leopard in Admiral Adam Duncan's Fleet. This ship was one of a number involved in the serious Mutiny of the Nore in May 1797. Hargood was put ashore by his crew. Following the end of the mutiny he was appointed on 12th July 1797 to the 64 Gun Ship HMS Nassau, joining Duncan's Fleet in the North Sea. On 23rd February 1798 he took command of the 64 Gun Ship HMS Intrepid on convoy duty to China after which he joined the East Indies Fleet under Vice-Admiral Peter Rainer until the spring 1803.

On the 23rd November 1803 he took command of the 74 Gun Ship HMS Bellisle and joined Nelson's Mediterranean Fleet off Toulon. He remained with Nelson watching the Toulon Harbour and formed part of the "Inshore Squadron". On the 12th May 1805 Hargood, in

Belleisle, formed part of Nelson's detached fleet that chased the French Fleet to the West Indies. Nelson returned in early July 1805, but Hargood was ordered to Plymouth and the Channel Fleet. He joined Admiral William Cornwallis off Brest but was immediately directed to refit the Bellisle at Plymouth. He rejoined Nelson's Fleet off Cadiz on the 10th October 1805 and took part in the Battle of Trafalgar. (6)

The Log of Bellisle from Monday am 21st October 1805 to noon Tuesday 22nd October 1805 gives a clear indication of the actions fought by Hargood and his crew. (7) Bellisle was part of the Lee Column under Vice-Admiral Cuthbert Collingwood. At one stage of the action Hargood engaged three enemy ships. Despite severe damage he took possession of the 80 Gun Spanish Ship Argonauta. The Bellisle was completely dismasted and was taken in tow by HMS Naiad and eventually reached Gibraltar. The Belleisle suffered heavy casualties: Two Lieutenants; One Midshipman; and 31 Seamen and Marines were killed; and 94 Seamen and Marines wounded. Hargood was himself injured being knocked over by a "splinter" and badly bruised from the neck to the waist.

After Trafalgar

Hargood was to receive the congratulations of his old shipmate Prince William, Duke of Clarence for his part in the Battle of Trafalgar. In a letter to Hargood headed, "Bushy House, Friday Night" he wrote: "I congratulate you from the bottom of my heart that you have at last had the opportunity of convincing your brother officers of those merits which I have long known you to possess. ...It is a matter of great satisfaction that my old shipmate is so well thought of". (8)

Hargood stayed in command of the Belleisle and after repairs at Plymouth rejoined her on 8th May 1806. On the 16th May 1806 he joined Rear-Admiral Strachan's squadron that searched for a French Squadron under Admiral Williaumez, said to have been making for the West Indies. (In Strachan's Squadron was Captain Sir Thomas Hardy in 74 Gun Ship HMS Triumph).

The squadron sailed to Barbados in search for Admiral Willaumez's but both the French and British ships were dispersed by a gale. A rendezvous had been previously been agreed by Strachan and his captains off Cape Henry. Here Hargood met with the 74 Gun Ship HMS Bellona and the 36 Gun Frigate HMS Melampus. They sighted a French Ship, Impetueux, under "jury rigging" headed for the neutral port of Chesapeake. Hargood chased this ship. Her captain ran her aground off Chesapeake. Hargood ordered the Melampus to fire on her and she struck. Despite being in neutral waters Hargood took possession, but on sighting some other sails ordered her to be burnt and for his ships to withdraw. (9)

Hargood returned home and transferred to the 74 Gun ship HMS Northumberland part of the Fleet that was blocking Lisbon in 1808. He then co-operated with the Austrian Army in the Adriatic in 1809 against the French. On the 28th March 1810 Hargood sailed for England in a now very leaky Northumberland in company with the 110 Gun Ship HMS Hibernia also in need of repairs. On the passage home Hargood was instructed to use his efforts to take under his "protection" five Spanish Ships of the Line at Carthagena. On the 23rd April 1810 he sailed for Gibraltar with 2 Spanish Three-Deckers, the Ferdinand V11th and San Carlos. Hargood eventually reached Spithead on 22nd June 1810.

He was promoted Rear-Admiral in on 7th August 1810 and in September 1810 as 2nd in Command at Portsmouth. On the 13th March 1811 he was in command of a Squadron off the Channel Islands, and on his return to England he married Maria Somers Cocks on the 11th May 1811. She was the third daughter of Thomas

Somers Cocks, Banker, of Charing Cross who resided in Downing St.

Hargood had another tour of sea duty from 29 March 1813 until May 1814 when he was appointed C in C Guernsey. He had his flag in HMS Vulture and during his command was successful in reducing piracy around the islands. He was promoted Vice-Admiral on the 4th June 1814 and in 1815 nominated KCB. With peace declared in 1815 he retired and moved round the South of England eventually buying a house in Bath in 1817. In 1817 Queen Charlotte accompanied by Prince William came to resided in Bath and the Prince and Hargood were to meet almost daily.

On the 22nd July 1830 he was promoted Admiral and in 1831, the Coronation Year of his old shipmate Prince William, he was nominated by the Prince to become a GCB and subsequently GCH. On the 27th Apr 1833 he was appointed C in C Devenport (Plymouth) a post he held until April 1836. (10) Here he met Princess Victoria and her mother the Duchess of Kent. In 1836 he moved back to Bath where he died on the 11th September 1839.

By a coincidence Hargood was connected by marriage to Admiral Sir James Nicoll Morris. Morris married an elder sister of Maria Somers Cocks, Hargood's wife. Both Hargood and Morris had fought at Trafalgar and were customers at Lock & Co.

Nelson Correspondence

Nelson correspondence with Hargood as recorded in the literature is not prolific. Two personal letters refer to professional matters. A memorandum of the 12th July 1804 from Nelson to Hargood asks him to be: "... be on your guard against a surprise of the Enemy, during your stay in Agincourt Sound, (11)

In a letter dated 1st July 1805 from Nelson on HMS Victory he tells

Hargood he had hoped to see him on board dining with him. He goes on: "..but I need not , I hope, assure you, how glad I am always to see you,...". Nelson had, as previously mentioned, met Hargood when they were both serving in the West Indies with Prince William. Nelson never forgot his Old shipmates and was always glad to have them with him, and Hargood was no exception. (12)

Hats from Lock & Co

HARGOOD Admiral Wm: 4 May 1811. (B113). 5 Bury Street. Round Hat 6½.
His first order was just before his wedding and perhaps was worn on his honeymoon.

HARGOOD Rear-Adml Wm: 10 Apr 1813. Portsmouth. Frock Naval Hat & Trimmings 6¾, Vellum Loop ⅜ In; Wood box.
This second order for a Naval Hat coincides with his appointment to the Squadron patrolling in the Channel Islands

HARGOOD Adml Wm: 18 Feb 1815. 9 St James's Place. Round Hat 6½ Full.
The last order, currently found, was placed at the time he had decided to retire.

References:

(1) Williams, Sir. E. DICTIONARY OF NATIONAL BIOGRAPHY. The Compact Edition. London: Oxford University Press, 1975. Vol 1. p896
(2) Allen, J. MEMOIRS OF THE LIFE AND SERVICES OF ADMIRAL SIR WILLIAM HARGOOD G.C.B.,G.C.H. Greenwich: Richardson H.S. MDCCCXL1. p2
(3) Allen. p7
(4) Allen. p22
(5) Allen. p30

(6) Nicolas Sir N. THE DISPATHCES AND LETTERS OF LORD NELSON. The Nicolas Edition. London: Chatham Publishing, 1998. Vol VII. p94 (Nicolas)
(7) Nicolas, Vol V11. p163-5
(8) Nicolas, Vol V11. pp311-2
(9) Clowes, W. L. THE ROYAL NAVY. A History from the Earliest Times to 1900. London: Chatham Publishing, 1997. Vol 5. p196. (Clowes)
(10) Clowes, Vol 6. p223
(11) Nicolas Vol V1. p109
(12) Nicolas Vol V1. p468

NAVAL HATS 1800-05

Locks have a unique record of the types of naval hats worn by some of the Officers of King George 111's Navy. With a few exceptions, the data covers the period the 1783-1815. The Admiralty Board introduced the first "Dress Regulations" on 14 April 1784. These attempted to bring some uniformity to the naval dress to be worn by officers, but did not mention hats. In the earlier years 1783-1795 hats were usually triangular in shape and the three sides being cocked, though bicorne hats were becoming more popular. These latter were worn either 'athwart', across the head, or front to back, 'fore and aft'. (1)

In June 1795 the Admiralty Board issued new regulations relating to the style of 'naval dress' to be worn by officers on different occasions, and instructions regarding the appropriate type of naval hat. By this time the hats were predominately bicorne in style. (2)

Flag Officers: Full Dress Uniform: To wear a Gold Laced Hat.
             Undress Uniform: No specific requirement other than it was to be a naval style of hat.
Captain 3 years Post: Full Dress Uniform: To wear a Gold Laced Hat.
             Undress Uniform: A Plain Hat.
Captains under 3 years Post and Commanders: As for Captains of 3 years post.

The regulations allowed all officers one year to conform. Additionally the regulations laid down the types of lace and buttons to be used on the hats. This was important, as Locks had to provide the correct pattern according to the officer's rank. The buttons were defined in regulations dated 1st October and 1st November 1787. (3) The regulations of 1 October 1787 stipulated that Flag Officers were to use a Gilt Button embossed with an anchor surrounded by a Laurel. The regulation of 1st November 1787 then stipulated that Captains were to use a Gilt Button with an anchor in an oval.

The button was an important part of the naval hat and held the Cockade to the side or front of the hat. The button had attached on the rear surface an integral screw and nut. The Cockade was centred in a loop of naval ribbon that fitted over it. The width of the ribbon varied according to the size of the cockade. The button then fastened through the cockade and loop into and through the side of the hat. The nut on the inside was tightened to hold the cockade firmly to the hat. King George 1 had first introduced the wearing of a cockade on naval hats. (4) The Dress Regulations attempted to bring some semblance of uniformity to naval dress and hats.

Locks' ledgers have limitations identifying the type of hats ordered, for example:
Identifying whether the hat ordered by a naval officer was bicorne or tricorne in shape. By 1800 most naval hats were of the bicorne style. (If bicorne whether the hat was to be made to be worn 'athwart' across the front of the head or 'for and aft' front to back). During the period 1790-1815 the bicorne hat was worn athwart.

During the period 1800-05 three types of naval hats were ordered: The Full Dress or Gold Laced Hat; Frock Hat; and Plain Cocked Hat with Cockade. The first and last type corresponded to the hats laid down in the 1795 Regulations. Both types were provided in a 'folding style' if required at no extra charge. The Frock Hat could also be provided in a folding style and will be discussed later.

The following account of the naval hats assumes the order was for a BICORNE STYLE OF HAT.

FULL DRESS HAT

Locks' ledgers variously describe this type of hat as: Full Dress Navy Hat; Full Uniform Hat with Gold Lace; Naval Uniform Hat with trimmings. In some orders the term 'silk hat' was added to indicate that a silk cover was placed over the crown of the hat, situated between to the two upright flaps. The hats were made from Beaver Fur dyed black and had two flaps. These were placed either side of the crown. The height of the flaps could vary according to the customer's wish. The flaps were stiffened to stand upright and termed 'cocked or cockt'. There were variations in the style of cocking the flaps as seen in portraits of officers of that period. Figure 11 illustrates a Full Dress Hat of the period based on the style of a civilian Kevenhuller Cocked Hat. Of historic interest, Lord Nelson never ordered a Full Dress Hat from Locks.

The Gold Lace required by the Admiralty Board was to be between 1½ and 2in wide. This was hand sewn onto the edges of the hat. Gold Lace was expensive and there were different patterns available. However, there was no regulation regarding its style. The width, style and complexity of sewing the Gold Lace to the hat determined the cost. The hat was usually lined with white silk unless otherwise requested. Locks inserted a company label and the duty patch to show the Hat Tax had been paid.

The trimmings for a Full Dress Hat were as follows:
Gold Tassels: There were usually two tassels attached one at each end that hung over the edge of the hat.
Gold Anchor Button: This was appropriate to the rank of the customer and was fixed by a screw to the hat.
Gold Laced Loop: The loop was made from felt or stiffened silk, usually silk. It went over the cockade and helped hold the cockade to the hat by the button. The Gold Lace was sewn onto the edges of the loop with Gold thread.
Cockade. This was usually made of navy blue silk and referred to as a black cockade.
The price of a Full Dress Hat varied between five to six guineas between 1800-05. This hat was ordered by all ranks of officers including Midshipmen.

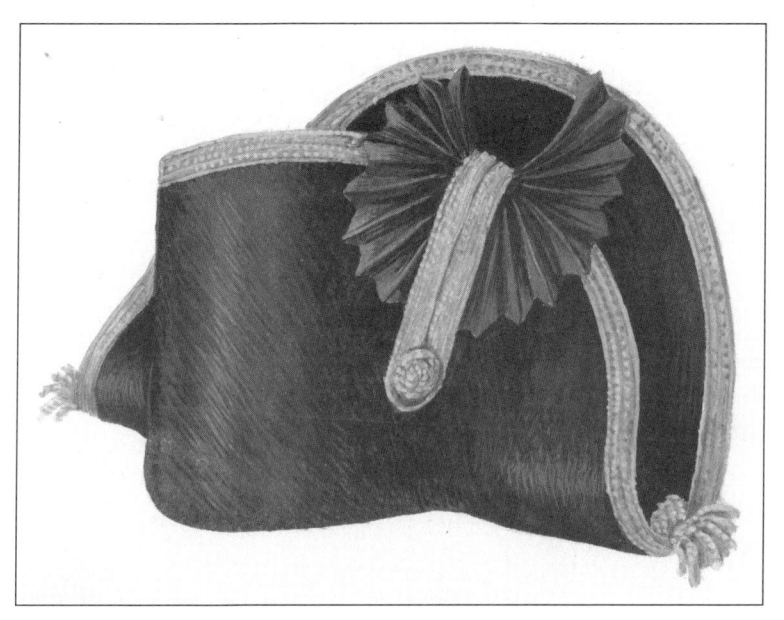

Figure 11: Full Uniform Hat.

PLAIN COCKED HAT

This was the commonest type of naval hat ordered. They were made from Beaver Fur and in the ledgers are referred to as a 'Cocked Hat & Cockade'. The price varied between 1/11/6 in 1800 to 2/12/0 by 1805. The loop and cockade were navy blue (referred to as black) in colour without any gold lacing. The button conformed to the Admiralty Board' pattern for the customer's rank and were black in colour. The ledgers show however, that despite the Admiralty Regulation requests were made by customers for trimmings to be added. The commonest was for the use of a gold button instead of plain black, and gold loop to hold the cockade.

FROCK NAVAL HAT

The origins of this term appear to relate back to the early part of the eighteenth century when the term 'frock' was used to denote a style of coat worn on ' common occasions'. The term was later replaced by 'undress uniform'. There are no records in the ledgers between 1783-96 of an order for a Frock Hat by naval officers. There are some for military officers. Prior to 1796 orders for naval hats were entered in the ledgers as "Beaver Hats and Cockades", with or without trimmings.

Orders for Frock Hats start after the 1795 Regulations. The orders indicate that this was not a 'Plain Hat nor a Full Dress' one. The style was intermediate and ordered by all ranks of officers. Basically the Frock Hat was the Plain Cocked Hat to which the customer then ordered his own style of trimmings. This is shown by the following orders:
Captain John Markham: 22 April 1796: Frock Naval Hat and Gold Lace band 2/2/6. The gold lace band was stitched round the edges of the hat.
Lieutenant John Clarke: HMS Inspector at Sheerness. A Frock Navy Hat and Gold trimmings, 2/2/6. The trimmings consisted of a Gold bordered Loop, Gold Button and Tassels. No lacing was ordered.

The 'folding style' of Frock Hat was occasionally ordered and the cost of such a hat was determined by the amount of trimmings requested, as shown by Admiral Whitshed's order:
Admiral Hawkins Whitshed: 12 July 1805: Frocked Folding Hat & Trimmings, Size 7½: 3/13/6.

Locks provided 'setts' of Naval Trimmings for the Full Dress and Frock Hats. In addition Locks prepared setts specially made up at the customers' request. The commonest order was for the basic Sett of Navy Trimmings. This consisted of: a Gold Navy Button according to rank; Gold Banding to sew onto the edges of the hat; Loop; and Cockade. For a Full Dress Hat the sett would include: Gold Tassels; Gold Lace instead of banding; and a Gold Edged Loop. The price varied between 1/12/6 to 2/2/- according to content.

Their remains one other hat which naval' officers regularly bought and was not in the Admiralty Regulations! This was the Round Hat, whether the simple style or the more elaborate Bedford or Thanet. This was the off duty civilian hat of all officers. They cost between 1/1/- and 1/7/6. (5)

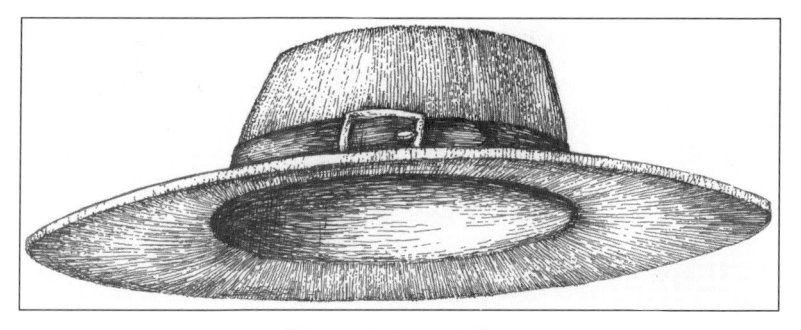

Figure 12: Round Hat.

REFERENCES

(1) Clowes, W. L. THE ROYAL NAVY. A History from the Earliest Times to 1900. London: Chatham Publishing, 1996, Vol 111. pp348-9 (Clowes)
(2) London Gazette 1795
(3) London Gazette 1787
(4) Clowes, Vol 111. p21
(5) Cliff, K.S. MR LOCK; HATTER TO LORD NELSON'S NAVY 1800-1805. Norwich: Wendy Webb Books, Norwich, 2000. pp77-83

ACKNOWLEDGEMENTS

The author wishes to acknowledge the kind help of Mr Ken Hutchinson who undertook the very fine drawings found in this booklet.

FIGURES

Figure 1: James Benning.

Figure 2: Flapt (Clerical) Hat.

Figure 3: Lord Nelsons Hat with Eyeshade (Worn at Trafalgar).

Figure 4: Lady Hamilton's Order.

Figure 5: Capt Blackwood's Order 1797.

Figure 6: Capt Capel's Order 1802.

Figure 7: Capt King's Order 1806.

Figure 8: Capt Hardy's Order 1808.

Figure 9: Capt Morris's Order 1806.

Figure 10: Capt Hargood.

Figure 11: Full Uniform Naval Hat.

Figure 12: Round Hat.